"I hope the reader finds this manual a useful tool
to help bring more blessings in both practice and teachings."
—JOHN TOMPKINS, JR.

THE REIKI PRACTITIONER'S GUIDEBOOK

This guidebook is for Reiki practitioners who want to expand their under-standing of how Reiki works with the energy of the human body. In addition to information on Reiki healing, it presents a thoughtful examination of the questions and issues that Reiki practitioners are likely to encounter.

Mastering Reiki includes unique discussions of Reiki history, the Reiki principles, the use of symbols within Reiki, and advancement through the Reiki degrees. For the Reiki instructor, it also provides a complete and accurate teaching program.

ABOUT THE AUTHOR

John Tompkins, Jr., has been a Reiki practitioner for eight years. Having attained the Reiki Master degree after a year of apprenticeship, for seven years he has been instructing students through lectures and Reiki workshops. Besides practicing Reiki, Mr. Tompkins is also an Espiritísta, doing readings for clients with a holistic approach, helping them understand the lessons behind their karma that is manifesting.

It is in Jacksonville, Florida, that Mr. Tompkins learned of the more effective and feasible form of medicine known as integrative medicine—medicine that uses both allopathic and holistic methods of treatment. Reiki energy, a valuable part of this treatment, proved effective not only on its own, but also as a compliment for those under allopathic care. Insights gained from spiritual methods like Reiki were also able to provide suggestions in not only physical but psychological management of challenges faced by patients. Mr. Tompkins now resides in Tennessee with his partner.

TO WRITE TO THE AUTHOR

If you wish to contact the author or would like more information about this book, please write to the author in care of Llewellyn Worldwide and we will forward your request. Both the author and publisher appreciate hearing from you and learning of your enjoyment of this book and how it has helped you. Llewellyn Worldwide cannot guarantee that every letter written to the author can be answered, but all will be forwarded. Please write to:

John Tompkins, Jr.
℅ Llewellyn Worldwide
P.O. Box 64383, Dept. 0-7387-0206-4
St. Paul, MN 55164-0383, U.S.A.

Please enclose a self-addressed stamped envelope for reply,
or $1.00 to cover costs. If outside U.S.A., enclose
international postal reply coupon.

Many of Llewellyn's authors have websites with additional information and resources. For more information, please visit our website at:

http://www.llewellyn.com

— *MASTERING* —
REIKI

A PRACTICING AND TEACHING PRIMER

JOHN TOMPKINS, JR.

2002
Llewellyn Publications
St. Paul, Minnesota 55164-0383, U.S.A.

FIRST EDITION
First Printing, 2002

Cover design by Gavin Dayton Duffy
Editing and book design by Rebecca Zins
Interior illustrations by Wendy Froshay

Library of Congress Cataloging-in-Publication Data
Tompkins, John, 1972-
    Mastering Reiki: a practicing and teaching primer / John Tompkins, Jr.—1st ed.
        p. cm.
    ISBN 0-7387-0206-4
    1. Reiki (Healing system)   I. Title.

RZ403.R45 T65 2002
615.8'51—dc21

2002016011

Llewellyn Worldwide does not participate in, endorse, or have any authority or responsibility concerning private business transactions between our authors and the public.
    All mail addressed to the author is forwarded but the publisher cannot, unless specifically instructed by the author, give out an address or phone number.
    Any Internet references contained in this work are current at publication time, but the publisher cannot guarantee that a specific location will continue to be maintained. Please refer to the publisher's website for links to authors' websites and other sources.

Llewellyn Publications
A Division of Llewellyn Worldwide, Ltd.
P.O. Box 64383, Dept. 0-7387-0206-4
St. Paul, MN 55164-0383, U.S.A.
www.llewellyn.com

Printed in the United States of America
on recycled paper

ACKNOWLEDGMENTS

First I would like to thank my patients and students for the material presented within this book, for each of you has been my greatest teacher of Reiki.

Thanks also to Mikao Usui, and to my own instructor/Master, Steven Greenstein, without whom any of this would be possible.

To Beth Hopkins, AP, who taught me to experience energy in new ways.

To Ann Bozzutto, a true mentor by example.

To my family, who think I'm a bit eccentric, but love me anyway.

To my ancestors and guides, who are always telling me what to do for my own good, even as stubborn as I am.

To my godparents, for helping to put me in line with my destiny.

And last, but not at all the least, to Bob Caylor for sharing his life, his love, and his support with me.

CONTENTS

INTRODUCTION

Reiki is a revolution. Why? Because although many other modalities have spread throughout the West as quickly as Reiki—such as herbalism and massage therapy—none have been as fully accessible to learn and use. With Reiki, there are no concerns for herb or drug interactions, no muscle manipulation, no requirement of months or years of anatomy education. It is practiced not only on the professional level, but all over the world in homes and healing places where men, women, and children are meeting in Reiki Circles or Reiki Shares in order to give and receive Reiki with one another for free.

The evolution of healthcare—both the changing of its definition and its return to the jurisdiction of the patient—is a very important part of our moving from the Piscean Age into the Age of Aquarius. In order for this transformation to be effective, however, and in order for us to retain responsibility regarding both its practice and its teaching, we must look toward both its spread and its evolution with a greater awareness. As a part of this, I would like to see Reiki continue to spread, as every student and instructor of a tradition hopes for their tradition to always grow in strength. Strength requires more than just numbers, however. It also requires curiosity, practice, study, determination, and honor. A tradition of one thousand weak followers has become a weak tradition, ineffective for even those within its fold. A tradition of twenty strong followers has remained a strong tradition, able to utilize its effectiveness both within its fold and with others.

Reiki is not only a revolution, it is also *undergoing* a revolution. It is at a critical point here in the West, as it tries to move in a proverbial ten thousand directions. There are many who are putting in hard work and long hours to make sure that Reiki continues to gain in strength and reputation . . . and there are others who are not so careful. *May there be only blessings for those on either side.* But it is up to each student and each teacher to decide which camp they are going to align with, or indecision will create that decision for us. We can show a strength, a responsibility, and an effectiveness that eventually cannot be denied by physicians, psychologists, and even insurance companies, thus taking our rightful place in integrative medicine along with other modalities such as massage, acupuncture, and naturopathy. However, we can also grow further in a direction of diluted teachings, irresponsibility, and disorganization, and continue to be passed over by the aforementioned professionals.

The conflict of allopathic medicine (Cartesian, treating separate facets of our multi-dimensional being) and holistic medicine (treating the entire organism: mind, body, and spirit) has proven to be unavoidable. It has been happening each and every day for a very long time. It is in the paper every morning, in the television news every evening, and faced every day by professionals on both sides of the fence. Like the revolutionaries of our past—those like Moses, Jesus, Orunmila, Krishna, Buddha, and Rumi—we must be the revolutionaries of *our* day, saying, "*That* doesn't have to be the only way! You've forgotten *this*!" It's not that the allopathic disciples aren't telling the truth. They're simply leaving out some very important parts! The laws by which they want us to abide—from the separation of flesh and spirit, to the mighty food pyramid—simply do not work. They fall short of the true definition of health—what we call *wholeness*. This is the reason behind the ongoing confrontation. It is not about which form of medicine is best, or which form should be practiced. Like the pressure between opposing plates within the earth creates mountains, so too does the friction between the two poles of medicine create a very important third entity. This is *integrative* medicine . . . a medicine in which both holistic and allopathic modalities are given a place of value and practice. Reiki, as a holistic form of medicine and spiritual growth, is a simple but effective part of this triad.

It is my sincere hope and prayer that this book will help fill a void that I, as well as other Reiki practitioners, have seen steadily growing for some time. It is a void within the practice of Reiki here in the West, and a void in the participation of Reiki among the other holistic healing modalities as these modalities grow in acceptance from their brothers and sisters in allopathic medicine. As a practitioner, Master, and teacher for approximately eight years, I can attest to the beautiful healing power of Reiki, not only by my own account, but also by the accounts of my clients and loved ones. The purpose of this manual is twofold, then: First is to provide a tool to help teach Reiki in a way that is easily comprehended. This will aid in creating more educated (and more correctly educated) practitioners and Masters. For example, correcting our teachings about Reiki's origins and energetic nature are indicative of the adjustments now gradually taking place within the Reiki community. Second (but not less important) is to help provide a format of teaching in which the integrity of Reiki may be more fully regained and preserved.

In the present we are seeing more and more "Masters" who are being produced en masse without these two most important factors: decent education, and preservation of the tradition's integrity. As a consequence, the Reiki community as a whole does not receive, nor can it command, the amount of respect drawn by other growing holistic healing modalities. There are several reasons why Reiki, as it is being taught and practiced today, has created a body that has failed to draw this recognition and respect, a few of which are as follows:

- Lack of sufficient education and experience among its practitioners.

- Lack of the same among its "Masters."

- Abundance of misinformation spread about Reiki's origin, definition, and practice.

- Lack of professionalism and focus within its practice in the West.

- Lack of purity within Reiki instruction, causing confusion among practitioners concerning what is and is not traditional Reiki practice.

As mentioned previously, I have been a Reiki practitioner, Master, and instructor for several years. One of the most important things that my Master taught me, and that I have since seen to be true, is that there is a difference between a master and a Master. A master has not yet overcome the aforementioned problems found within the tradition as practiced here in the West, and indeed may not even be perceptive enough to realize that these *are* problems, leading to even greater problems both for the individual practitioner and for the entire community itself. A Master has faced whichever of these obstacles existed for her, and has overcome them through awareness, dedication, and experience.

This is not only the seed of the problem but the solution, I believe, for the Reiki community. In no other tradition may someone go to a weekend seminar and leave with the right to call himself "Master." (Of course, no one should be receiving all three degrees in a weekend in the first place, no matter what the third degree is called. Those who say that it's okay because they were a special case should realize just how many "special cases" are being produced these days.) In all other traditions, whether from the martial arts of the East or the trade guilds of the West, it takes *years* of actual experience before one may be considered to have earned the title of Master. This is an important factor for our community to face and reconsider, for our perception of who we consider to be the Masters of our field must change if we are ever to deserve the respect our tradition once had among other healers and healing professions. Mikao Usui was a respected healer of his time . . . how many of our "Masters" have earned the same respect? It is because of this that I prefer to consider myself a "Reiki III" or "Reiki instructor," as I encourage of the handful of students I have taken to this degree. Unfortunately, however, we in the West have named this degree "Master," rather than giving the name to those with the experience, and it is spread that one must be a Reiki Master in order to pass the attunements that advance a person to the next Reiki degree. Thus, I must call myself a Reiki Master when doing public speaking, teaching, or writing in order to show that I have the required training/degree. The contradiction between the title and its true definition should be rectified as our community continues to advance more and more students to this degree.

Reiki is a wonderful tradition, and a positive tool that benefits all living beings on this planet. This book is meant to address the growing challenges that the tradition is facing. Thus, tools to aid in positive transformation through awareness and information are also provided in order to give an accurate portrayal of both the practice of Reiki here in the West and of how we may reestablish a balance. Positive intention is imperative to the health of the tradition, but good intention can still bring darkness when carried by either lack, or inaccuracy, of information—this has been the case as of late. I believe, however, that universal truth eventually wins over common misinformation, and the truth of our own energy systems is as close as our own bodies.

Everyone from student to Master should find this book useful. For the Master, a program for teaching has been suggested, and new insight and opinion has been offered regarding many elements of our tradition. Students may find it a gentle guide, perhaps to find some information or clarification that they may feel is not being received from within their own lineage alone. I, personally, encourage my students to enjoy speaking with and learning from other students and Masters by listening to their new perspectives and personal cases. It can be an invaluable tool for us to learn from one another, and particularly from elders within any tradition. Sometimes added information may be gleaned; sometimes it serves to simply make us more grateful for the teachers we already have.

As a final note, symbols will not be shown within this manual. Traditionally the symbols to use are those that have been handed down by the Master who has advanced the student to that degree. I have no desire to detour from that tradition here, nor do I care to either tout my lineage's version of the symbols as *the* correct version or defend them from others who regard their own lineage's symbols as such. Hand positions are treated in a similar way, with illustrations of suggested positions given with the understanding that there are great variations within different lineages.

With these things in mind, I hope that the reader finds this manual a useful tool to help bring more blessings in both practice and teaching.

CHAPTER I

REDEFINING REIKI

The first thing most of us asked as students of Reiki was, "What *is* Reiki?" It is a sensible question for one in this position, and most of us received the same two answers. The first answer is our famous four-word definition of Reiki energy as "Universal Life Force Energy." Then we receive some version of Reiki's origin, which may contain varying degrees of factual information. Both parts of Reiki's definition, being important, deserve further exploration.

REDEFINING REIKI ENERGY

We were taught that Universal Life Force Energy, and a particular method of utilizing it for healing, is Reiki. Most likely, our teacher went on to define this energy as the same phenomena observed in the East and named chi, ki, or prana. Certainly, these are all forms of energy, all branches or streams of the one energy that pervades the entire universe . . . but is Reiki really the same as these?

The most simple reply, based upon what has been traditionally taught to us in the West, is yes. The correct response, however, based upon actual observation, is a definite no. This may not be what many practitioners have been taught, but in reality it is based upon one of the most important principles and behaviors of the Reiki energy: Reiki never harms. Any acupuncturist, shiatsu practitioner, or yogi will tell you that chi, ki, and prana are not so predictable. Many people who have an understanding of Reiki believe that they, too, have an understanding of chi, ki, and prana, but it is incorrect to assume this. Healing utilizing the latter three forms of energy is much more complex, and is the reason behind years of study prior to opening practice. In order to better understand these terms, as opposed to Reiki, one must consider the following.

Chi, ki, or prana (known as *Ra* by the ancient Egyptians, or Kamitians) are names for raw life energy. Much like fire, this is not innately "helpful" or "harmful," "healthy" or "unhealthy." Rather, it is the *balance* of this energy that creates health, and *imbalance* that creates disease. It is also important to note that not only too little, but also too much, of this energy can create death or disease. It is also possible to have both excess and deficiency coexisting within the same subject.

To make this difference more clear, and to understand the profoundness of it, we can create an example case scenario. In the practice of Reiki, if a patient comes to us with difficulty due to heart problems, we would do a treatment on the individual with special attention given to the placement of our hands upon the area of the heart, sending extra energy to this location. The intent is that the energy infuses this area well and speeds healing and recovery.

In working with chi, however, depending on the diagnosis, it is quite possible that this would worsen the patient a great deal. For someone working with a patient's chi, such as a Qi Gong practitioner, it would be important to first note whether the patient is dealing with *deficient* or *excess* chi within the heart region. A patient with an enlarged heart due to excess buildup of chi would be harmed a great deal by strengthening the buildup of chi in that area. Instead, a release of that chi, either by purging or perhaps by redirecting it to other networks of the body that show deficiency, would be necessary. Thus, in utilization of Reiki, extra energy given is always going to have a positive effect, while in working with chi proper education must be acquired in order to avoid danger to the patient.

Prana can be equally tricky. The raising of prana through the *sushumna*, or central energy channel along the spine, is a worthy endeavor. Balance must be kept, however, as this is done; and one must be prepared to face the issues within whatever blockages are released. Both physical and mental damage can occur by undergoing the process alone and without care, and this is why the scriptures and yogis are strict about having the aid of a Master for this process.

Thus, the most frequently taught definition of Reiki is indeed accurate, but incomplete. An acupuncturist, who is also a teacher and friend, told me once that she did not understand how Reiki could be practiced by so many individuals with no understanding of chi and its different natures and behaviors. She had been told the traditional definition of Reiki, which caused in her a misunderstanding of the nature of Reiki, just as it usually causes a misunderstanding of chi in most Reiki students.

What, then, would be a more accurate definition of Reiki? If Reiki is Universal Life Force Energy (ULE), but doesn't act like other forms of ULE, then how can we better view, define, or depict it? I liken it to the somewhat Catholic concept of grace. Grace is nothing we can earn or deserve; God is just always there *giving* it. Certainly God's energy is everywhere, but grace is that really nice component, as opposed to some of them that aren't always going to do what we want (like the energy forming a hurricane). I have heard others liken it to love. Yet others have likened it to intelligence, because of this very difference: it always knows what to do and where to go.

It is possible that another one-line definition can't accurately depict the ULE known as Reiki, as opposed to the other vibrational levels of ULE. Perhaps descriptions, case stories, and shared personal feelings do a much better job. Reiki practitioners are fortunate in our opportunity to utilize and teach a modality with very few boundaries or restrictions, and no reason to fear that it will be "done wrong." We are able to boast that it is always harmless and always beneficial, like love. This difference is more than simply worth noting, it is worth *teaching*, because it is central to our practice. For when we are engaging in this activity, we are infusing ourselves and our patients with this very energy, and the difference that it is always safe, always positive, is a source of comfort to both.

REDEFINING REIKI'S ORIGINS

A number of legends arise with the birth of any great venture. Many are true, and some not so true. But it can be said that most any myth is based upon truth, the truth of which may be found if one looks hard enough. This certainly applies to the birth of Reiki. Reiki has seen the emergence of many versions of many stories that claim to describe its origin.

There are certain things we have no way of knowing regarding the origin of Reiki. We have no proof, first of all, that Reiki was ever practiced at any time other than modern day. Many claim that Reiki was *re*discovered by Mikao Usui, but this is a claim for which we have no proof. There is also a school of thought that Reiki was once practiced in an extended, more complete version in ages before history as we know it. Often this story is precluded by claims that it was brought to our planet by other beings. One particularly popular myth is that Reiki's origins are within Tibetan Buddhism, commonly practiced by monks (conveniently located in mountains far away).

What is the truth? Is there any way of knowing for sure? I would say that the only thing we know for sure is that the truth becomes what we choose . . . and is often much more poetic than the cold, hard facts. The most common elements of the story that describes the birth of Reiki as we know it today are as follows.

In the early 1900s, in the city of Kyoto, Japan, lived a man by the name of Mikao Usui. It is said that Usui was a Christian, and a teacher at a Christian school for boys. Upon being asked by his students to explain the healing miracles of Jesus, he decided to search for the answer. It is said that his search lasted several years, first in his own country and within his own religion's scriptures. When this failed, it is said that he traveled to the United States to learn further. After still not finding the answers he was looking for, Usui returned to Japan to speak with the Buddhist monks there. The monks seemed to no longer be interested in matters of healing the physical body, but allowed Usui to stay and study *sutras* (scriptures) himself, in search of the ancient methods of healing.

Within the sutras, it is said that Usui felt that he had found the answers to what he was looking for, except for how to actually put the knowledge to use. According to legend, he therefore decided that he would go to the top of Mt. Kurama to fast and meditate for twenty-one days, in hopes of reaching that understanding. Usui created a pile of twenty-one stones; each day, he cast one stone. Finally, just before dawn of the last day, as Usui was about to cast his last stone, he perceived a light coming quickly toward him from the sky. It is said that Usui's first response was to run, but he caught himself and decided that he would stay to receive what was coming for him. The light struck Usui in the third eye, and he saw many bubbles of light before him. It is within these bubbles that Mikao Usui was shown the Reiki symbols, and in which their meaning and use was revealed.

Excited, Usui rushed down the side of the mountain—and split his toe on a stone. But when Usui put his hands on his toe, the wound healed! This is considered the first miracle. The next miracle came when he went to a nearby inn to finally have some food. It is said that the innkeeper tried to persuade Usui not to eat so much food directly after a fast, as it invariably causes great discomfort. Usui would not listen, evidently, which was the cause of the second miracle: no discomfort.

The miracles kept rolling in on that fateful day. The innkeeper's daughter, it is said, had a toothache, which at that point had made her entire jaw swell. Being very poor, the innkeeper had no money to take his daughter to a dentist. No problem. When Usui fixed that, he gave us the third miracle (and probably got his lunch for free). Usui then continued on to one of the monasteries, where he met a monk with terrible arthritis. It is said that Usui healed the monk of his arthritis, and provided us with the fourth and last miracle of that day.

The next few years were spent healing beggars in the streets of Kyoto. Usui became disillusioned, however, when he noticed many of the people regain health, and yet go back to begging even though there was no longer anything preventing them from being able to work. It is said that he then realized that providing Reiki without expecting payment in return created a situation in which it was undervalued.

This is where the story of the origin of Reiki tends to end. Separating the fact from the fiction would be difficult, if not impossible. There are certain things that we do know, however. One is that Usui did exist, and did found Reiki. Mikao Usui was born August 15, 1865, in the village of Taniani, Gifu District, Japan. A monument exists on Mt. Kurama, where he had his experience that enlightened him of Reiki. Knowledge of the body's energy systems, and various forms of healing with that energy (such as Qi Gong), would have been commonplace. Reiki certainly fits nicely with the traditional oriental medical teachings (such as TCM, or Traditional Chinese Medicine) that have ancient roots back to Taoism, but obviously it has its own equally Buddhist parentage.

We also know that Usui opened a school in Tokyo in 1922, to teach the Reiki method. Many students were trained, but only sixteen were brought to the level of Master before his death on March 9, 1926. One of these students was Dr. Chujiro Hayashi, who studied under Usui in 1925. Hayashi made several reforms to the system, and it is he who then taught Hawayo Takata. Takata was first a patient in one of the Reiki clinics, but after being healed insisted upon learning Reiki herself. Hayashi was reluctant at first, because Takata was a foreigner (from Hawaii), but eventually agreed to teach Takata, who received her Mastership in 1938. Takata then opened her own clinic in Hawaii, and is thus credited with bringing Reiki to the West. It is through Takata that most practitioners in the West trace their lineage.

These are some of the few cold, hard facts. No records have been found regarding Usui having ever attended school in the States, and certainly no one can validate another's spiritual experience any more than one can *in*validate one. With the understanding that nothing happens by accident, however, we may find that there is a great deal to learn from the one version that has become a part of our tradition.

Mikao Usui's journey is really no different from the spiritual journeys of us all. Big questions begin to appear out of nowhere, and the journey begins. He begins at home, then searches far and wide . . . only to realize that his answers are surely found back at home. Asking others provides little or no help, only alternating moments of discouragement and encouragement. In reality, we can only find what we are truly looking for by being still and searching within. Of course, when the answers come, they challenge us where we stand, and we have the choice to either run or to receive them.

Most of us get excited when we first sense progress. This is what Usui did. He ran and, although he knew where he wanted to go, he forgot to pay attention to his own footing. Unless we take care of our own grounding first, we will fail at our ability to help others. Thus the first miracle provides our first lesson. *Take care of things where you are before taking the next step, consciously.*

Of course, Usui didn't have to be reminded twice. When he got to the inn, his next step was again one in which he took care of himself. He knew he was in a weakened state, and thus did what was natural, strengthening himself. This is "healer, heal thyself" being illustrated for us. *We cannot attempt to facilitate healing in others if we are not keeping ourselves in good health.*

The gastro-intestinal area is also, metaphysically, an area that symbolizes assimilation of new things. *Once we take care of things where we are, we must assimilate knowledge, experience, etc., because we cannot offer what we have not yet assimilated ourselves.* This is where the lesson of the innkeeper's daughter comes in. With a swollen jaw caused by a toothache, the daughter is unable to assimilate physical nourishment. Taken into symbolic language, this would be an obvious reference to spiritual nourishment. Usui's action showed two things: First, it is an example of the correct order. Usui had taken time for his own spiritual assimilation, and then helped the daughter with hers. Second, it is an illustration of the point that *we must help our patients and students in such a way that they gain in self-sufficiency in order for it to be true healing.* When Usui was finished, the girl was able to take in nourishment herself.

By Usui returning to the monastery in which he had done so much study, and healing the monk of arthritic pain, we are shown the importance of several points. The first is *respect toward our elders.* Those who have been on a spiritual path before us, even if it is a different one, have wisdom to offer us from experience they have gained through their own seeking. Also shown is the importance of *remaining open to receiving help.* We were not placed on this planet alone, and there are many parts that make up a healthy environment. The monk, as a spiritual elder, knew this. Too many times, those who become teachers try to either create a pedestal-like status or uphold one that the students have made for them. What is detrimental to the teacher, though, tends to be detrimental to the student. Also, the strongest way for us to teach is by the example we give our students through the way we live our lives. We cannot expect students to be open to receiving help when offered, if we are not doing so ourselves. After all, we cannot expect students to become healthy Masters in areas where we have only exemplified disturbance.

In redefining the origin of Reiki, it may prove worthwhile to separate fact from a great deal of fiction. To be respectful, we cannot further misinformation or make claims more grand than we can stand behind. Many may *wish* that we had a Tibetan origin, or that Reiki was brought to us by the gods themselves. But continuing to create and further such invalid claims serves only to broadcast some strange neurosis in which our own Masters are dissatisfied with Reiki's true beginnings. In reality, this is unwarranted. Reiki was born of an individual whose culture and studies would have afforded him extensive knowledge of the human energy system. Further study taught him about yet another way to practice healing, while spiritual revelation activated the energy in him, also allowing him to pass it on to others. This is very similar to the introduction of other forms of both healing and martial arts.

Thus, the need to separate fact from fiction must be faced . . . and yet, as mentioned before, every tradition has its legends. Often these parables teach truth in ways that the simple cold, hard facts overlook. This has been utilized in every faith throughout the world. In our traditional story of its origin, Reiki benefits from both this kind of teaching and from the important facts still being passed down. If we can continue to hold this balance, then the history and integrity of Reiki will be preserved.

CHAPTER 2

USING THE REIKI PRINCIPLES AS OUR FOUNDATION

I remember when I first started organizing my Reiki information into a structure more feasible for seminars. Like anything else, this is an ongoing process. We are never done learning, and so we can never be done finding new ways to improve our teaching. The most difficult part, though, is organizing it for the first time; after that, it will grow and change with the individual practitioner or Master. But how does one do this? Giving Reiki treatments, and even attunements, becomes an integral part of the practitioner or Master, like breathing. I also had to clarify to myself which parts of my healing work were actually Reiki, and which parts of it were made up of other modalities in which I was also experienced.

Even my own training offered little clarity. Of the several things my Master taught me, I had to figure out what was truly Reiki and what were his own views on Reiki, as well as other modalities altogether. My searching was done through two methods that I used simultaneously. One was to carefully try to inventory both what I currently did during my sessions and what I could remember my Master sitting down and teaching me. Within that inventory, I narrowed down what I knew pertained only to Reiki. The other method I utilized was meditation. I felt that in order to do the best job possible, I needed to receive help from my highest guidance. The intent was to gain input as to what new students of Reiki, and any form of energy work, needed to know in order to have a firm foundation upon which to practice.

The method was a success. During the process, I felt like a human funnel. I would receive instruction even in my sleep, awakening to hear voices trailing off in my head. Channeled over a two-week period was the blueprint of a foundation strong in every respect, with the exception of the experience that each student would have to earn over time. Included was everything from Reiki history, taking care of the energy system, the major chakras within the body, Reiki procedures, to hands-on experience. The first seminar was a success, and I thanked my guides profusely.

During that period, I remember that just about *everything* came into question. There was so much I wanted to teach my students that I knew I had to weed out anything unimportant in order to cover everything I wanted to. One of the first things I questioned was the teaching of the Reiki Principles. I had seen too many healers put faith in affirmations without concern for the actual root of their own or their patient's difficulties to have much faith in them. I also felt that, as the Principles were rather elementary points, they seemed a bit too much like taking my adult students back to kindergarten. So, of course, I took this into meditation.

"Do I really have to teach them?" I asked. "If they're really traditional, and not just wishy-washy, then what are they for?"

The answer I received was immediate and strong.

THE CULTIVATION OF ENERGY: THE REIKI PRINCIPLES

The amount of energy we have can be decreased or increased. According to traditional oriental teachings, this energy comes in two forms. One form is the energy we are born with. This is the energy passed down to us through our heritage, which contributes to a healthy birth. The other form is the energy that we take in. By cultivating and maximizing the energy we take in through sources such as food, air, and sunlight, we need draw less from the limited amount that was passed down to us. The amount and balance of energy within us then contributes not only to our physical health, but to our very perception of the world around us.

This is where the Reiki Principles come in. Regardless of what model of energy system one tends to agree most with, the cultivation of our energy is known to be an important endeavor in the teachings of all such models across the globe. The Reiki Principles usually consist of the following:

Just for today, I will give thanks for my many blessings.

Just for today, I will not worry.

Just for today, I will not be angry.

Just for today, I will do my work honestly.

Just for today, I will be kind to my neighbor, and to every living thing.

There is a common function that is served by living each the above affirmations: the development of chi. In our Western culture, we quickly see that living in the above manner is beneficial to the collective, usually having been taught the biblical golden rule or Ten Commandments as a way of being kind to others. Every spiritual tradition has its own expectations of upright behavior from its followers. This, then, was not the point that Usui or his descendants were attempting to make, as it would be redundant to students who already have such expectations from their various faiths.

We know, then, that the point of the Principles is not for the benefit of the collective, but for the development of the individual. *In every tradition based upon the flow of energy, the healthy cultivation of that energy is the central goal.* The martial arts Master does not act in a conscious, collected manner because it is an expectation, but because it is living in a conscious manner that effectively builds chi. The building of chi is important because everything he does is based upon its flow; it is projected through his art form, his healing, his vitality (and therefore health), as well as his spiritual awareness and abilities. A Master has cultivated his chi for many years through careful, deliberate action and nonaction. Areas that waste, deplete, or destroy chi are avoided.

A Reiki Master or practitioner must be aware of the same consequences of his actions and inaction. Although Reiki is a beneficial energy, spending a great deal of time channeling this energy to help others is still very demanding on our own bodies and energy systems. It is said that the more one does Reiki, the more the power grows in the practitioner. After years of experience, I definitely believe this to be true. The attunements serve to open up the practitioner, but if the workload is demanding, the practitioner has the responsibility to strengthen her vessel and pathways to take on such stress.

If a practitioner chooses to create a lifestyle that builds, rather than diminishes, her energy, she must live more consciously than those who are not energy workers. This includes an internal responsibility every bit as much as an external one; perhaps more. It is within the state of inner peace that energy can grow and mature. Living in a way where emotional excess is allowed depletes and destroys the energy already within the practitioner. Emotions, it is said, are adequate slaves, but poor masters.

The five Reiki Principles, then, are important internal points where the cultivation of our energy stands.

The First Principle: Giving Thanks for Our Many Blessings

The First Principle works because living within a state of gratefulness is essential to providing an inner environment that nurtures and attracts both inner *and* outer abundance. In other words, being thankful for what we already have is a powerful first step to creating and attracting more. This is true of both outer and inner resources of energy. It is also important because if we take for granted what we have, we will be less attentive in its development, whether we are speaking of our material well-being, our relationships, or our energy. In fact, we *have* a relationship with our energy, whether we realize it or not. Not realizing it is, basically, taking it for granted, which prevents us from consciously developing it.

The Second Principle: Releasing Worry

The Second Principle is probably one that many healers address early in their practice. It is no coincidence that so many healers have had a great number of challenges to work through. If we chose our destiny as healers, then we probably also chose a path that would give us the best tools possible with which to do the job. The opportunity to face the wounds within ourselves first is perhaps the best tool we can claim. Those of us who had to face many problems early in life learned to be hypersensitive to any signals or possibilities of problems arising. We always expected it and looked for it. Thus we learn to worry, and the fact that we are now working with the emotional challenges of others seems to give us all the more reason to continue to do so.

Of course the reason is a false one. Worrying about the patient is certainly not going to be as effective as holding a positive vibration as we offer a hand to help. And worry, like anger, has its own particular danger: It hides. Worry can become chronic to the point that a chronic worrier may not even realize that they worry too much. Worry is an energy drain, and constant worry means a constant wasting of energy. This lost energy cannot be built, and this chronic wasting away can lead to deficiency and fatigue. If I could say there was one opposite to worry, it would be faith. True faith is not blind; it is the realization that the universe is already set up to help us, to work for our highest good. This offers strength, as opposed to the worry that would weaken us.

The Third Principle: Choosing Not to Be Angry

The Third Principle works in a similar manner. Anger can waste a great deal of our energy in huge bursts. It also, however, can become chronic. When it becomes chronic, it acts in a very different way than worry. When someone begins to carry anger around inside, the energy actually begins to turn in upon the owner himself, even if the anger is toward others. Anger attacks the very carrier, often causing chronic pain. This tends to produce guarding, or tightening of the muscles, which then leads to even more pain. Blood pressure may rise, and a whole host of problems ensue. Therefore, energy is not just lost, but what is still contained becomes unhealthy and turns upon the owner. What is needed may include some mixture of forgiveness, relaxation, or just learning to let things be, perhaps leading toward anger's most powerful opponent, peace.

I met a Master who had problems with this Principle. Her issue was that she had a right to feel her anger. What we are looking at, however, is not the attempt to suppress our feelings, but taking the responsibility to learn to respond in more healthy ways in the first place. Taking care of volatile situations is necessary; responding to them in anger is not. It is possible to learn to stand our ground in a more calm, collected manner. This is true even if at times we fall short, particularly regarding matters or people that we feel deeply about. Doing so, we find that we can remain at least as effective as before, yet without producing, carrying, and throwing destructive energy. There is a difference between reacting and acting; one is a behavior in which we allow others to dictate our actions or emotions, while the other is action consciously decided upon by ourselves. In the first choice, we give our power over to others, while in the second, we keep it for ourselves.

The Fourth Principle: Living Honestly

The Fourth Principle teaches us about the result of our own character upon our energy system. Honor is held in our gut; it is there that we know what is honorable or dishonorable. If we cheat another, we know it and we are robbed of a part of our energy. If we lie, the same thing occurs. We know what does and does not uphold truth, and we cannot build our energy upon a false foundation. When we know that our word means nothing, and that we cannot even trust ourselves, then we cannot view ourselves as powerful beings because we know that our words and our honor must have standing. This prevents us from being able to build our energy until these situations are rectified. Then, as honor is built in our solar plexus, the energy can be regained as well.

The Fifth Principle: Growing Kindness

The Fifth Principle teaches us the lesson of reciprocity. To believe we cannot possibly harm another without also harming the greater whole mandates the belief that we, too, are then harmed. Quantum physics is making great strides in proving this very law. This can also be looked at from the old metaphysical laws that "evil begets evil" or "evil turns upon itself." We have already noted one way that this can occur as we looked at the effects of dishonor upon our energy system. The opposite is also true, however, in that good creates more good, or positive energy builds more positive energy. Anyone who has tried to change their own thinking patterns knows this. When we learn to see the glass as half full instead of half empty, our life seems to take a better turn. If this is true—that good begets more good—then simply taking positive steps of kindness toward our neighbors should cultivate more positive energy within us, as well as in the world. In fact, those of us who practice Reiki have already found this to be true.

"Just for Today"—The Empowering Phrase

Metaphysically, any time the same words are repeated three times, a point is trying to be made—someone is attempting an act of power. Three times is supposed to be enough to get the point through to all parts of us: conscious, subconscious, and superconscious; mind, emotion, and spirit; body, mind, and spirit—there are a number of ways we can separate our awareness into a trinity. The fact that "just for today" is stated at the beginning of every Principle, then, shows that it holds some importance sufficient to warrant such repetition. After all, it didn't *have* to be done that way.

Just for today holds a power that makes us more likely to succeed in living each of the five Reiki Principles. Twelve-step programs know this, placing great importance on taking things one day at a time. If I am trying to *never* anger or worry again, then the burden is perceived as being much larger, and that perception then *makes* it larger, and I am much more likely to fail. *Just for today* limits the goal to one I feel more capable of handling; if not, I can always shorten the increment to *for the next five minutes* or even *right now* (this one can be particularly helpful when stressful situations arise, such as long lines or someone cutting us off in traffic).

Just for today also retains the power in another way. It keeps us more focused on the present—after all, we only have power in the present. This does not mean that we cannot *affect* the past or future, but to do so we must still take our action (i.e., send or cultivate the energy) in the *present*. One of the most common ways we disempower ourselves is by living in either the past or the future. But we have no power there; we temporarily gave up that power when we chose to incarnate within a construction in which time is affected by relativity.

The five Reiki Principles, then, are a strong base upon which we may build our energy. They lend themselves not only to our inner cultivation of energy, but to keeping ourselves powerful in other facets of our life as well. Being a student of Reiki is not simply receiving the attunements. This simply puts one on the path. It is also a lifetime of learning to utilize that energy. Being a Reiki *Master* means continuing down that same path as we take on the added responsibility of teaching it.

— CHAPTER 3 —

ADVANCEMENT THROUGH THE DEGREES

One of the most important matters of ethics to be considered at this time regards the advancement of students to their first or next degrees. The viewpoint that is quickly gaining the majority of the Reiki populace is that, since Reiki is for everyone, advancement through the Reiki degrees is something to be done both automatically and without deliberation. Simple math explains this phenomenon; make more students and Masters haphazardly, and the number of Masters, in turn, haphazardly cranking out yet more Reiki students and Masters will grow exponentially. The history of Reiki and a look at other healing arts will show, however, that this mode of transmission was never intended, and had instead been rather carefully prevented.

There are many kinds of traditions that in time will, and should, change as the consciousness of the populace expands, usually under the provocation and leadership of a few who are advanced in an area far ahead of the rest. Such traditions already seeing such transformation include the restriction of participation in many areas by women, minorities, and the economically disadvantaged; restriction of freedom such as the freedom to choose one's spouse or partner; or unequal value of representation in society or courts of law to minorities. Reiki itself has seen a breakdown of several of these traditions, with the initiation of Hawayo Takata and the increased availability of Reiki to the economically disadvantaged in the West. Adequate time spent for the advancement and education of each student, however, is a tradition that should never be sacrificed in Reiki, nor is it being sacrificed in the other healing arts.

A popular argument is that "the Earth needs more healers," and that the more healers, the better. This argument, evidently, entitles a Master to line up students in a row of chairs and give the attunements to all of them at once. Another opinion held is that Reiki was once in the hands of the few, and that teaching Reiki in a much less mass-oriented manner is nothing more than an attempt for the same "few" to keep Reiki for themselves. Both arguments carry a great deal of validity. Unfortunately, attempting to correct these issues by swinging the pendulum from one extreme end to the other creates at least as many problems . . . simply from the opposite extreme. Interestingly enough, either way we run an equal risk of losing the Reiki tradition. Once the risk was from sheer lack of numbers during a war; now it is by lack of actual cultivation of the tradition by those who have it.

Such a risk may seem incredible to some, but our society already has a history of diluting other spiritual traditions, until finally contributing to their scarcity. How many well-intentioned individuals are now professing to practice some form of Native American spirituality? This is a prime example of where mass-producing spirituality may truly lead its followers. Quality, not quantity, is what must be intended if any tradition is to be truly preserved. If no one holds the actual understanding of a tradition, then that understanding cannot be passed on to future generations. The power that comes with such understanding is then lost and, worse yet, so is the wisdom gained through countless years of experience. Dreamcatchers with plastic parts and flipping cards to find one's animal guides are symbols of lost effectiveness in such a version. The number of keepers of the true Native traditions (or even the languages) is dwindling, even on the reservations, even though it is predominantly these keepers who still hold any true power.

In Reiki, we now have our own version of plastic dreamcatchers, our own Masters who teach shortcuts for advancement parallel to flipping cards in order to find one's power animals. Catering to the ego—or what one wants to hear—will always produce more money. Telling what *needs* to be heard—that effort is required—will always make one unpopular. However, one is an act of power and one is not; in Reiki, as in all else, one receives what one puts into it. All healing traditions, as traditions that deal with energy, know this. One cannot go to a weekend seminar and be considered experienced in Qi Gong, or be titled a black belt overnight, whether all the stances are learned or not. Neither can one be called a Master of Tai Chi just because the entire form has been learned. And yet we in Reiki continue to make people "Masters" in a weekend, giving them the authority to teach a method that they have only utilized, at best, a handful of times. Yes, we need more healers—but this includes allopathic doctors, acupuncture physicians, nurses, naturopaths, and all other kinds of healers, all of whom require time in which to adequately learn their field.

TIME FOR CHANGES

Aside from simply gaining further experience, time between degrees allows for yet another positive process to occur within the Reiki student. The Reiki attunement is not a magical process in which all of the blockages within an individual suddenly disappear—not any more than during a treatment. During both an attunement and a treatment, blockages within the individual are being broken up or dislodged. I liken the energy to the flow of water within a hose, or blood within the veins. When such blockages and *ama* (buildup) are broken loose, *they have to go somewhere. They still have to be released.* Release still happens through natural processes. This is why people may cry, laugh, forgive, receive closure regarding events, feel extreme peace, or have any other number of experiences from a treatment or attunement. This is also why, in Reiki, *students see their lives change.* It is law that as above, so below, and as within, also without. The world outside of us is both an extension and a mirror of that which is already within us. Thus, as changes take place within us through healing treatments, we truly find that our life changes externally as well. We simply attract and create another reality around us. This is even more powerful and more noticeable when one receives an attunement.

An attunement dislodges a much greater amount of blockages, in order to clear the way for more Reiki energy to be available to the student. Because of this, the student is offered even more opportunity to grow from the experience. This often translates into an experience that the student may later regard as a turning point at which his life began to move on to another level. Often, guidance is gradually felt more greatly, family life makes long-needed changes, and a further satisfaction and peace with life on Earth as it is grows within the student.

Certainly, these changes can be facilitated without ample time being given between attunements. I do believe, however, that the experience is greatened by such time being taken. Personally, I would never choose to trade my experience for another, simply because it may have taken time. I took some extra time between my First and Second Degrees, more than my Master thought necessary. There was less time between my Second and Master Degrees, and my Master and I both felt that I was ready. There is no pattern to follow. A shorter amount of time does not mean that one student is more advanced spiritually than another; nor does a longer period mean that a student is slow to learn. It simply means that one student's experience is different from another's . . . for *whatever* reason. Time is only relevant to the ego, not to the development of power.

EXPERIENCE

It can and will be argued that Reiki works automatically and thus negates the need for experience to gain advancement. It is true that Reiki works automatically, as far as the energy itself. Positive energy will always have a positive effect. However, only those who do not understand both the amount of good a good healer can do and the amount of harm a poor one can *also* do could ever argue such a point. I have seen both situations occur plenty of times. I have seen patients whose T cells have skyrocketed as the result of receiving Reiki treatments, and seen health restored in limbs. I have also, however, seen a Master who was confused about her own use of Reiki, and thus was incapable of clearly explaining the use of the Second Degree symbols to a student she was advancing. I have witnessed a Master start right in with the Freudian "tell me about your childhood . . . you had a bad one, with problems with your mother" script on an already psychologically damaged patient, whose childhood was both happy and healthy. I have also known a Master who still had not overcome difficult sexual issues within his second chakra, and made inappropriate advances toward at least two of his own students.

These kinds of things happen. These kinds of things happen *much more frequently* when attention is not paid to the readiness for advancement of prospective students. Reiki is a form of energy healing, and as such it will always attract a high percentage of people who are in some way already very sensitive to energy, whether they know this or not. It is also a community that attracts a large number of people who would often be considered very spiritual. Those who are aware that they are on a spiritual path are usually working with their energy in a faster, more intense manner, if simply through their own intent. This choice dictates a reality in which issues come up more quickly and intensely in order to be dealt with so that spiritual advancement continues to occur at a quickened pace. Most of us in the West grow up in a society that fosters messages that actually run counter to spiritual growth. This means that as our energy rises and expands, there are plenty of areas in which we must find balance and harmony, transforming the negative suggestions that we have internalized. In some areas, we will find this fast and easy. At other times it will create a real struggle, and that struggle can manifest in an infinite number of internal and external power plays. Sometimes, we go through difficult patches in which we seem to be manifesting unhealth as opposed to health, no matter what we do. In reality, it may simply be the process of healing, as the source of imbalance is being purged from our system so that the balance may replace it.

Experience often outweighs the importance of timing when considering the advancement of a student. A massage therapist who received his previous Reiki degree six months ago and uses Reiki every day will have more experience than a student who received his degree a year ago and has not utilized Reiki since. The knowledge and wisdom that can be gained only through application within real-life circumstances is far more important than any amount of time that may be predetermined by a practitioner's lineage. Thus, to students who want to rush through the process, I tend to recommend a minimum amount of time to process and work with the changes that occur within each degree; and yet I am open to the fact that a uniform time table for advancement cannot possibly fit something so inherently unique as personal experience. Usually I am a bit insistent about students having at least six months of using their previously earned Reiki degree before continuing on to the next. This is very safe, as even if there is no "spiritual" reason why they should not continue forward, it gives them more time to actually grow into their role as a Reiki I or Reiki II before continuing on to the next desired degree. For example, taking someone very quickly from Reiki II to Reiki III would mean that they never even had the time to learn what living as a Reiki II is all about, or what it is like giving a treatment as a Reiki II. How, then, can they teach or discuss it well? Remember also that many people will not be ready to advance for an even greater amount of time, or perhaps not at all. The degrees are different in the roles they play, but different is not the same as better.

ALIGNMENT WITH LIFE CYCLES

As demonstrated by the previous scenarios, spiritual growth through awareness is not easy . . . if it were, more people would be doing it instead of either giving it over to some external deity or choosing to continue to be blissfully unaware to begin with. This is something to be considered when choosing to take on or advance a Reiki student. For example, the first thing I do when assessing a prospective Reiki student is look at their energy flow. Are they aware that the attunement will act in a manner in which blockages are removed? Are they ready for that process to be sped up? For example: A student going through a divorce may feel that he has enough on their plate for the time being, and may choose to wait until later, to aid in the healing process at that time. Of course, another in the same situation may view it differently, feeling as though the majority of issues were worked through before the divorce was decided upon, and that now is a time in which extending healing to both parties would be particularly beneficial.

If I see large obstructions in a person's energy flow, I ask them to go home first, and meditate (or simply sit still) and ask the question whether or not this is the right time for them to receive the attunement. Usually, we will both receive the same answer. Often, I receive an answer that is not what I would expect. In this case, it is sometimes the answer for me to attune an individual that I would not have wanted to attune. The reason tends to be made known later, such as a relative entering the hospital soon after the attunement, or difficult issues that the individual will soon be dealing with.

KARMA

Another pertinent point to consider is whether or not the student is ready to take on the repercussions at this time. One thing that was not made known to me while a student, and which most students are never taught, is that receiving Reiki degrees "speeds up" one's karma. When receiving a Reiki attunement, the amount of energy of a particular vibration that the student channels is increased. Increased energy means a larger responsibility to use that energy correctly and wisely. A greatened ability to be of help means more situations in which one *must* help—it is one less excuse to turn one's face the other direction and ignore the suffering of others. To put it simply, the question "Am I my brother's keeper?" increasingly becomes "Yes." We will always have the responsibility to respect another's autonomy, and yet we also have an increasing responsibility to be of help the more we are given the gift to do so. Hence my saying that karma is sped up. For what is karma but responsibility for one's actions, even if often over lifetimes?

GROUNDING

Yet another important factor to look for in a student is whether or not they are well grounded. This seems to be at a premium. Reiki is a high, buzzing energy, and thus tends to attract those who are high, buzzing people. Of course, this is a wonderful energy, important as any other. But to be only on this end of the energy spectrum is imbalanced. For some people, it is simply indicative of a particular point in their lives. Many of us in our younger years were more than willing to give up the benefits of being grounded in order to live what we viewed a more "happy go lucky" or "free" lifestyle . . . only to learn later that lack of focus can just as easily bring limits to our "fun" life. For others, though, lack of grounding is not necessarily a phase that they consciously entered into. Abuse, hypersensitivity, and dissatisfaction with the decision to live in the first place are all reasons that may contribute to a lack of grounding that starts early in life as a defense, and which the individual may find very difficult to reverse later on.

While many in the pursuit of quickening spiritual growth are trying to raise their energy vibration, many of us involved with Reiki have primarily the opposite challenge: to learn to better ground ourselves. Lack of grounding creates problematic situations due to symptoms such as lack of focus, difficulty staying centered, loss of energy, difficulty dealing with immediate situations, avoidance in dealing with one's own issues, and gaps in communicating clearly with others who are more grounded. There are far too many Reiki students and Masters today who have a far-off look in their eyes and a lack of cultivation of their own energy. I refuse to advance someone to the Reiki Master Degree who still has difficulty grounding, not out of prejudice but out of fairness to the student. I feel that this problem should be dealt with first, and then the Reiki Master Degree be considered.

Reiki energy does not ground an individual. Anyone who has ever experienced a Reiki treatment knows this. Reiki is an expansive energy and, without balancing it with contraction, the mind becomes dispersed with the energy flow, and is just as difficult to collect and refocus as the energy itself. The same is true for the practitioner. Because of this, Reiki makes it more, rather than less, difficult to ground. This is why learning to ground and cultivate one's energy is imperative for the Reiki practitioner. It is also why allowing a student to finish the course of Reiki degrees before learning to ground is putting the cart before the horse. In every ancient tradition based upon the flow of energy, grounding is taught before other utilizations of energy, through stance and/or meditation.

So how can we learn to ground? There are many methods available, some more effective than others. For the most part, visualization methods are not the best, nor are many of the popular meditation techniques. The goal is to move the excess energy from the higher energy centers to the lower ones, creating a balance in the body and psyche. Such a top-heavy imbalance can occur not just from being wishy-washy, but also from stress, worry, living too much in your head, and even too much intellectual activity that has not been balanced by physical activity. Visualization techniques (such as imagining oneself to become a tree with roots) still keep the majority of energy in the head, particularly in the *Ajna* (third eye) chakra. Tai Chi, Qi Gong, and forms of Hatha yoga, however, are acceptable forms of grounding, and are very effective ones. Tai Chi and Qi Gong are based upon the movement of the body and development of its energies, particularly the generating and building of it within the Sea of Chi (below the navel). Hatha yoga uses stretches to release energy blockages within the body while utilizing breathing and meditative techniques.

The theme here should be obvious: We are looking at proper use of the body, with our attention collected and focused on the present. Our soma is on the physical plane, even when our mind is not rooted in the here and now. If Tai Chi, Qi Gong, or yoga are not available or acceptable to you (or in addition to them), I strongly suggest gardening or landscaping. In addition to the physical exercise, we are also given the opportunity to merge with the earth, getting more used to its feel. By noticing more of its beauty, we may learn through experience that grounding into this plane can be a beautiful, safe experience. It is also a return to the Earth, from which we are used to taking so much more energy than we give.

INDIVIDUAL GROWTH

Expectations do rise with each degree. However, expectations should be based upon observation of the individual, not upon a desired mold for the masses. What is expected is growth, not a preconceived notion of what that growth would be. Otherwise, how could we offer advancement from one degree to the next to those students who are already beyond our own level of growth? In a perfect world, we could say that all people who are to be advanced to the level of Reiki Master will be nonsmokers, meditators, have a superb understanding of the human energy system, be able to utilize stones and herbs, and be talented in counseling their clients. The reality, however, is that there are many powerful healers who smoke (unfortunately, for those of us who would like to convince our students otherwise!), who couldn't council a client out of a paper bag, and who do nothing but lay on hands, pray, or whatever it is that they do. Some of the most powerful healing occurs, after all, from the simple act of just *getting out of the way*.

Thus, advancement is an individual affair, for which growth is the predominant expectation. One student may appear to grow more than another by outward signs, only for us to find that the *true* growth, that silent understanding and maturing within of the healer's own abilities, has happened in far greater strides in the person who has outwardly said or changed the least.

It is this requirement that gets people. It is more likely that I will pass a Reiki I attunement than a Reiki II. It is far more likely that I will pass a Reiki II attunement than a Reiki Master attunement. A student with whom I have no past history can still be expected to have a history of growth and it is that which I will listen to. What are the daily habits of the individual? Do I see that they are prone to anger or judgment? What are the personal care habits? If the student does not take care of herself, then she cannot tell another how to do so. Students cannot be blamed for turning out Masters no greater than themselves. It is important, then, to remember that when we advance a student, the effects do not stop with that particular student.

EXCHANGE

Reiki is anything but in the hands of the few these days, although there are still a few who will charge astronomical prices for the attainment of Reiki degrees. Interestingly enough, some of these individuals are the same people who shortchange the students on time and teach the most nontraditional forms of Reiki.

I disagree that money should be a determining factor in the decision whether or not to take on a student or advance them a degree. It took me, as it does many, a long time to learn the importance of exchange for my time, effort, and skill—even longer to become comfortable with accepting that exchange in monetary form. Exchange is a beautiful cycle, and being open to its many forms only adds to the beauty and blessings that one can experience in life.

My Reiki degrees were made possible to me through a man on a karma-yoga walk. He shared his teachings in exchange for what individuals were capable of giving him, taking food and lodging wherever he found himself. At that time, short periods of food and lodging were basically all I was able to give, and it provided an important lesson for me. I knew later that I would never turn away a student based upon an inability to give monetary exchange. Unless a student offers a suggested form, I don't let them worry about it, letting them know that some kind of exchange always seems to occur. Years later, I have experienced exchange in the form of clothing, transportation, education, meals, and the knowledge that I helped preserve the life and health of others, often children.

There is wisdom in the saying that only those who pay for Reiki will understand the value of it. Often when we give in return, we then understand more the value of what we were first given. "Payment," however, doesn't have to be monetary payment, although there should be no negative connotation toward this form, either. Money allows food, clothing, and a place to stay. At times, although I would still have appreciated food, I was glad to receive monetary payment because I already had food in my apartment, but still needed to make the rent.

I teach my students to never turn someone away due to lack of funds, and to accept other forms of exchange. I also challenge others to do the same, whether practitioners for treatments they give, or Masters for their attunements and teaching. There is nothing more empty than spilling your heart to teach someone well and receiving a check from someone to whom it means very little. And there is nothing more fulfilling than spilling your heart and receiving a home-cooked meal from someone who went out on a limb to do it because they truly appreciate your gift.

— CHAPTER 4 —

UNDERSTANDING ENERGY AND THE BODY

Having an understanding of energy and its manifestation of and within the human body is not necessary for the practice of Reiki. I would be remiss, and it would be misleading, if I did not make this known. There are quite a few Reiki practitioners who simply put their hands on or near their patients' bodies and then let the energy take over from there, unaware and uninterested in what is happening within. Obviously, this cannot be considered a bad thing. Spirit can do the most wonderful things if we are only willing to step out of the way. This, then, is an adequate and valid way of practicing Reiki.

GOING FURTHER

Why, then, go further? Why do many of us want to learn more, making the conscious study of energy a lifelong process? Simple fascination not withstanding, the answer is actually in the results. A session with the Reiki practitioner previously described may be as equally effective as a session with a practitioner who has extensive knowledge of the human energy system. A practitioner who has this knowledge, though, will be able to understand what is going on within her patient's energy system, and offer suggestions to the patient based upon this that might prove helpful. This, in turn, aids the patient in being a more active participant in the self-healing process. This is because doing so not only speeds recovery, but often helps patients better understand the roots of their dis-ease.

For example, suppose that patient "Bill" goes to the practitioner who has an understanding of the energy system. Bill looks a bit tired, and offers that he has been putting in a bit more work at the office the last couple of days, which has probably caused this condition. He is hoping that a Reiki treatment will help to perk him back up, since it has always worked in the past. During the treatment, however, our practitioner notices that Bill's solar plexus has an almost empty feeling, in addition to a low energy reserve in his kidneys and *tan tien* (the major energy center located approximately two inches below the navel). Based upon these findings, our practitioner intuits that Bill hasn't just been spending "a bit" more time at the office for just a couple of days, and that he hasn't been taking the time to eat regularly and properly.

Although he physically appears to others to be much better off than he is, she knows that Bill is about to crash in a big way. Knowing the importance of asserting the positive, she simply tells Bill what is happening in his energy system, and suggests that it is important that he stop burning the candle at both ends. She also stresses the importance of replenishing his energy through a healthier diet. Taking time to stop and do deep breathing every once in a while is also suggested as a way to drop some of the constant stress, and also to help build some more energy by taking in prana down to the tan tien and solar plexus. Bill admits that he has actually been working until late most nights for about two weeks, and that he hadn't really thought much about the skipped meals being replaced by trips to the vending machines. He agrees to put a time cap as to how long he will stay, make an attempt to eat better, and try the deep-breathing exercises. This puts him ahead, instead of falling behind, by his next Reiki treatment.

Most of us want to maximize our sessions with patients. Anything we can do to help them *maintain* better health is also desirable—and also what holistic healthcare is all about. Receiving Reiki treatments is a step in the right direction, but by offering feedback gained from the patient's energy system, they will understand how to better *take action* to work through imbalances unique to their own inner environment. Not everyone has the same needs in order to achieve the healing they desire.

The practitioner who wants to utilize an awareness of how energy manifests in the physical and emotional bodies of the individual must understand this. He must also understand two very important aspects pertaining to energy. One aspect is the nature of energy itself; the other aspect is a system that maps the energy's manifestations within the body.

One of the most common symbols of polarity is the yin-yang symbol. Equally important,
each emerging from the other, yin is the dark, contractive, feminine principle;
yang is the light, expansive, masculine principle.

There is no longer any question whether or not our body is composed of, runs on, and emits energy. We know that every atom contains electrical charges and fields. Being composed of so many atoms, it is obvious that we, too, must then contain and utilize a great amount of electricity—in our heartbeat, for example. How other electromagnetic fields affect our own energy—something already understood by sages—is still being tested by scientists, particularly those in the medical field.

POLARITY

Hot or cold, strong or weak, yin or yang: These are ways in which we express the polarities of our energy. A magnet has a northern, negative pole and a southern, positive pole. In the same way, our own body runs its energy in positive and negative polarities. This was known at least as far back as ancient Egypt. The ancient Egyptians called the energy within our body *Ra-Bhuto*. This same energy is depicted as emerging from the brow of the pharaohs in the form of a vulture and a serpent. The vulture, Nekhebet, refers to the electromagnetic-negative, cooler energy at the left side of the body. The serpent, Uachet, refers to the electromagnetic-positive, hot energy at the right side of the body. Their emergence at the brow of a pharaoh pointed to the fact that he—as every pharaoh—had gone through the initiatory training, raising his Ra-Bhuto (Indian *kundalini*) from its resting place (the base chakra).

It is important to remember that polarities are inherently relative, because the polarity is often the first quality noticed when working on a patient. For example, in comparison to another patient, someone may seem to have a much weaker energy, but in comparison to what their own energy was before, they may actually be much stronger. The same patient that we compared to, however, may actually be much weaker in comparison to their own previous energy, even though they are stronger than the first patient. Thus, at first an inexperienced energy worker may believe Patient A to be in decline, while Patient B is doing well . . . but, in reality, Patient A is recovering quite nicely, while Patient B is the one in decline.

Similarly, one patient may have a system that seems very yang compared to another system, but if the system we compared it to has an excess of yin, then it only makes sense that a healthy yang would seem excessive when compared to it. For example, a very strong heart chakra may seem overpowering next to a weaker, underdeveloped solar plexus chakra, calling for further work within the solar plexus. If the problem, however, had been due to an aggressive heart chakra instead of an underdeveloped solar plexus, then the imbalance would need to be corrected primarily by releases that would calm the heart chakra. Either way, the solar plexus is perceived to hold a lesser amount of energy. When compared to the rest of the system, though, we would see that in the first situation it is the solar plexus that is too yin, while in the second situation it is the heart chakra that is too yang.

ENERGY SYSTEMS

This information takes on further dimensions when we look at it within the framework of how energy manifests in the body. Having such a map is important because energy manifests as the mental, emotional, spiritual, and physical characteristics of each individual in a unique manner. When able to observe which energy centers or systems are being thrown into imbalance, we are able to know more about the ways in which an individual manifests and furthers the aforementioned characteristics. Once this is identified, the practitioner and patient may, together, come up with a better plan of recovery.

The model of information used matters very little, as long as it is one that *works* well. The most commonly used models tend to be the chakra system, some kind of traditional oriental system such as acupuncture or shiatsu, or a combination of two or more of these. Obviously, an acupuncturist would do best to utilize a TCM model from which to gain his information (such as the meridians and five elements), at least until gaining sufficient knowledge of a different model. Then he may draw upon the knowledge of *both* models. Likewise, someone who is used to meditation upon the chakra centers would do best to stick with this model to find his way around the patient, until gaining sufficient knowledge elsewhere. The phrase "until gaining sufficient knowledge" is important here. Misdiagnosis may not seem like an important issue within the context of Reiki but, again, this could only be argued by those still unaware of the equal effect both "good" and "bad" healers can have.

Obviously, when speaking of diagnosis/misdiagnosis, we are speaking of the "diagnosis" of what is going on within the patient's energy system. Legally, a Reiki practitioner does not have the right or authority to diagnose illness or conditions, whether mental, emotional, or physical. Speaking of diagnosis instead, then, as *an awareness of what is going on within the energy system,* it still holds a powerful effect upon the healing of the individual. This happens in at least two ways. One way is how this awareness will affect the faith, viewpoint, and motivation of the patient. This factor, which all healthcare workers know well, has a direct impact upon the healing of the subject and, in fact, may prove to be the most important factor of all. The other way in which a misdiagnosis may affect a patient, even within the practice of Reiki, is through the changes the patient tries to make in his life in order to positively transform unhealthy energy patterns on both the internal and external level. Remember, *we are asking people to take what is found in their energy system and actively utilize that information in such a way as to help further their healing.* A misdiagnosis could mean taking action that may actually be contrary, rather than complimentary, to the patient's healing.

To better illustrate this, we may take another look at one of our previous examples. Suppose the patient with the underdeveloped solar plexus had endured a childhood of abuse, with her primary defense to shut down and shy away from life (not an uncommon response). Her well-developed heart, however, is due to the consistent cultivation of positive intention, which she always shows others and is learning to do for herself. By reading her energy system, we already see the need for development of her solar plexus. And so it is suggested that she learn more about her inner courage by exploring her ability to be unafraid of living life and by attempting to stand strong for herself more often. These exercises are things that will help strengthen her solar plexus and return energy to it between sessions.

A misreading of her system, however, could have much the opposite effect. The assumption that the heart chakra was too yang, for example, would prompt a different cultivation of energy. The advice given may then be to back off from people, being careful about being too forceful, and remembering that at times she must take more care not to force her own emotions on other people as she becomes too carried away with situations. Because of the misdiagnosis, then, she is given a program in which her fear of assertiveness becomes even greater, and energy continues to be depleted from her solar plexus. The abused has just been miscast as the abuser. She then becomes dependent on Reiki, acupuncture, etc., to recharge her solar plexus energy instead of learning to hold and cultivate that energy herself. In this situation, she is left treating the symptoms rather than getting to the root of the problem. Thus, she would have done better seeing a practitioner without any knowledge of the energy system at all. Such a practitioner could then provide the Reiki and let the healing occur without obstruction as the patient more slowly made the necessary life changes herself.

In the end, the patient still has the opportunity to heal; we can't take that away from them. And even a setback may eventually become the steppingstone on which to move forward. It is our responsibility, however, to provide an environment in which the current opportunity to heal is maximized. As Reiki practitioners, we have a wonderful tool to bring into that environment. It is an oversight, though, to think that Reiki is all that we bring to the table, and to believe it is to deny the responsibility we have to use our other capabilities in a responsible manner. Our intention, emotions, words, and physical space are some other factors that we utilize when we are working on our patients; and it is our responsibility to keep them clear of chaos, negativity, or anything else that may affect our work.

GAINING THE EXPERIENCE

It is because of this commitment to care, safety, and optimal environment that we must address where to start the First Degree student. What energy system is taught, and how will they best learn about it? I can only offer advice based upon what I have seen generate success among my own students. For the energy system, I strongly recommend a basic teaching of the chakras, predominantly including the seven major chakras along the sushumna. This provides a sufficient map to facilitate great healing, where issues are brought to the awareness of the patient and/or practitioner in a clear manner, within the shortest amount of clinical and study time. This also addresses our second question: how to learn. *Everyone* is capable of going within and experiencing the chakra system through guided meditation, whether guided by another or self-guided at home. Thus, I start the students by having them take a look at their own energy system. The practitioner may then go "chakra diving" as often as she wishes, particularly in daily meditation. Doing so, she gets to know herself on a deeper level at the same time as learning what chakras feel like, how she finds it easiest to go inside and perceive them, and what kinds of things she might observe in them. By allowing the students to work on themselves and each other before moving on to other patients, they gain an assurance that puts both them and their patients more at ease, facilitating better sessions.

THE LEARNING PROCESS:
FROM WITHIN TO WITHOUT, LISTEN, MEDITATE, ACT

I begin, then, by giving the students a basic teaching of each of the seven major chakras, including handouts so that they may later study them at home and find them more easily within their body. I then have them do a short meditation with their eyes closed as they are sitting in their chairs (back straight, feet flat on the ground). I ask them to delve inside each chakra, beginning with the base chakra and ending with the crown. By the end of the meditation, every student knows what it feels like to observe from within the chakras. They also know which chakras they may like to work on more within themselves, allowing the healer another tool with which to keep their own energy system in better balance. The meditation is always enjoyed, and so easy that they feel comfortable doing it at home on their own.

Once a part of the class is reached in which the students have all done the chakra meditation and been attuned, I have the students work on each other. They are more comfortable knowing that they are all in the same situation, beginning to learn to understand the energy system of another based upon what is intuitively felt within the energy centers, the chakras. Everyone has a turn working on someone they do not know, and then receiving the Reiki from the same person. Time is allowed for the partners to share what they experienced from both positions. Generally students are unafraid to share with the class their own experiences receiving the Reiki treatments, and they are often amazed at the information they are capable of picking up from the person they are working on.

The next chapter provides some basic information on the chakras, including some pages that are in a handout formation that Masters may choose to copy for their students. Remember that this is a very simple, very brief primer in order to help students find their way around. If one studies the chakras for a lifetime, then they will have a lifetime in which they continue to learn more about them. Study from texts, a guru, and meditation are all recommended for further learning. Included are also chakra worksheets (one for before the chakra meditation, one for after), and worksheets for giving and receiving Reiki. This allows students to really think through what their own process was like. Doing so, they may also help others understand what to expect when undergoing a Reiki session that they will give.

CHAPTER 5

CHAKRA THEORY AND REIKI HAND POSITIONS

Before addressing the qualities of chakras, it is important to first have a clear understanding of what a chakra is. Many may think this obvious but, in reality, the myriad of answers one may receive only proves that too many do not actually have such an accurate understanding. For example, to define a chakra as one of the seven major energy centers within the body shows but one misconception that is all too common in the West. Conflicting information regarding location and correspondences of the chakras only make reaching a sound concept all the more difficult. Beginning with a simple, basic context is important, allowing one to progress from there both by experience gained from meditation, and from those who have accessed such knowledge before us.

Regarding a simple, accurate definition, we can say that *a chakra is an energy vortex.* That is all. There are actually *many* of these little vortexes all over the body (and beyond), varying in size and specific function. Interestingly, there are chakras within the feet, the hands, off the midline of the body, moving up the forehead, and many other places that people would often not guess. This knowledge comes from the sages and healers of literally thousands of years ago, who obtained this knowledge either from another even older civilization, or by their own observations over many years. With this understanding and definition of the chakras, we can even consider the oriental acupuncture/acupressure points to be chakras, as well as the several centers utilized by the Yorubas of Nigeria. And, although we are most familiar with the chakras as passed down to us in some form from Indian culture, it is evident that the ancient Egyptians had this knowledge as well.

FUNCTION

All of these little vortexes have the similar function of taking in and releasing the energy in our body, as well as relaying that energy between themselves. Our health (physical, mental, emotional, and spiritual) has an effect on their actions and efficiency, as does our environment. For example, around our most intimate friends, family, and partners, our chakras tend to be quite open; but if someone we do not trust enters the room, we tend to "close off" more. This expression has its roots in reality, as this is *exactly* what happens on the chakra level. It is also possible to not only close off our chakras, but to further open them as well. For the most part, any act of love will do this. This often includes acts such as meditation, healing sessions, creative expression, taking care of another person, and forgiveness of others or oneself.

Energy flows between the chakras through the *nadis*, or energy pathways, which are much like their physical counterpart, the nervous system. The three strongest pathways are the *ida*, *pingala*, and *sushumna*. The sushumna is the central channel that connects the seven major chakras as it travels from the base chakra all the way through to the crown chakra. Its diameter is affected by the amount of energy being channeled and the state of spiritual development of the individual. The ida and pingala are the channels that rise on the left and right sides of the sushumna, manifesting physically as the breath as it flows through the left and right nostrils. Keeping the nadis, like the chakras, clear and free-flowing is essential for health. Obstruction of this energy flow causes sickness and infirmity on all levels.

The chakras within the body have correspondences that may be used as tools to aid in accessing and bringing balance to them. The most common correspondences are colors, organ systems, musical tones, mantras, deities (spiritual forces), and stones. There are also herbal and astrological correspondences, as well as correspondences to age. These latter are usually used to better tailor healing curriculum to the individual by experienced healers, particularly those learned in Ayurveda. Another correspondence is utilized during visualization of the chakras as flower buds, each chakra being a flower with a different number of petals. Chakras are also often visualized as colored spheres or gemstones.

LOCATION

In order to make it easier on the student, we will be concentrating on only the seven major chakras found along the midline of the body. We will keep in mind that there are actually many chakras within the body and, in fact, continuing on for eternity above and below the body (becoming increasingly difficult to observe). It is often said that these seven major chakras are found along the spinal column. Many actually disagree with this statement, saying that the chakras vary in this alignment, some actually being found more *outside* the body than within. I suspect that the confusion comes from the fact that the chakras—like the rest of our body's systems—manifest on more than one plane, thus manifesting in more than one locale. Either way, for our purposes it is effective to work with the chakras as though they manifest along the spine. As much as alignment can be argued, it is what the practitioner finds effective that he or she must use.

Another matter of discrepancy is regarding the spleen chakra. There are quite a few individuals who call the solar plexus chakra the spleen chakra, using the terms interchangeably, with the belief that they are one and the same. I concur with Leadbetter and many others who do not consider them to be the same chakra, and it has been my experience within the healing context that it is not so. Because of this, I teach the solar plexus chakra within its traditional context, and do not teach about the spleen chakra when addressing only the seven major ones. These are addressed in the pages that follow.

FIRST (BASE) CHAKRA

Location: Perineum

Color: Red

Key Words: Security, Grounding, Group Identification, Initiation, Stability

Security and survival issues are found here. Any kind of abuse or neglect will have effects on this chakra; there is often referral, or connection, between one affected chakra and this one.

As the center that attaches and vibrates most strongly with the earth/physical, this chakra aids in keeping us grounded, i.e., focused in the here and now. Often emotional trauma will cause defense mechanisms such as vacantly "floating out there somewhere," or being constantly distracted by external events that do not directly pertain to oneself. Due to feeling that they cannot deal with their issues, these patients have found a way to avoid doing so. However, they will continue to be less effective in their lives until they learn to confront their issues and deal with life as it really is.

Part of our ability to ground, however, is based upon our feeling that we have some-thing to ground *to*. As such, feelings of belonging and acceptance are necessary. It is the difference between feeling, and thus acting, as a bystander, and being an active, effective participant/co-creator in life.

The term "initiation" is also included, in part, for this reason as well. The kundalini is stored at the base chakra, and moves upward from there. As we grow and blockages are removed, more and more of that energy is able to be released and move upward through the channels along the spine. Thus growth begins here, with the self, and every initiation we undergo must be firmly rooted in a healthy first chakra. Security in one-self must either remain constant or be regained as issues are dealt with while kundalini rises upward along the spine. Security in oneself cannot truly be gained from others, but often the situations in which we live or were raised will contribute to that feeling of security or insecurity, which is to be either cultivated or challenged.

SECOND (SENSUAL) CHAKRA

Location: Two finger widths below navel

Color: Orange

Key Words: Sensuality, Sexuality, Creativity, Generate, Cultivate

It is in the second chakra that we find our true beliefs, freedoms, or restrictions regarding sensuality and sexuality (this chakra is often called the "sexual chakra"). This is because it is the chakra through which we express our partnership with others within a more personal relationship, as opposed to the group dynamic handled within the first chakra. This does not include only those with whom we feel particularly intimate, or even close. It could be our boss, our child, or even a particular coworker when engaged with them outside of a group context. It is within the context of lovers, however, that we usually begin to experience the true power and intensity that is available when this level of intimacy and trust is heightened. It is this yearning for union that has sparked poetry, mystical rites, and meditation itself as methods to attain union with the Divine. In Western culture it is sometimes seen as heretical to depict or view the Divine from the sensual perspective, but it has not always been so around the globe. In most cultures, it is understood that our sexual longing is simply a manifestation of that longing for the Divine. As such, a healthy second chakra would allow an even greater, closer relationship with the Divine, however we view Him or Her.

It is also important, however, for a healer to note the creative and energy-building aspects of this chakra that are far too often overlooked. Creative energy is important in helping us to devise new and more effective forms of treatment for our patients and ourselves. This center, corresponding with the TCM concept of the "Sea of Chi," is a reserve that stores so much of the body's energies that it is important we work often on this area in ourselves, building the energy there and thus keeping ourselves strong. The same is true for those of our patients who are either often low in vitality or require a great deal of energy in order to facilitate their healing.

THIRD (SOLAR PLEXUS) CHAKRA

Location: Between navel and joining of the ribs

Color: Yellow

Key Words: Vitality, Willpower, Personal Power, Honor, Personal Identification, Self-Esteem

This chakra is vital in generating enough inner strength for continuing health within the body. Ebbs and flows here will often accompany or foreshadow changes in a client's health status. Often, when such warning is given, the problem can be rectified through proper nutrition, rest, exercise, or meditation.

The key words given above are all very interrelated. The balance of power is strongly affected by one's sense of honor. By aligning one's will with the will of the Divine, one does not have to worry about the temptation to inappropriately exert one's own will over another; nor does one feel a need to allow the opposite scenario (being stepped on) in fear of standing up for oneself. In this way, willpower and personal power (the appropriate use of willpower) may be cultivated, and the same honor that allowed this strengthening is itself strengthened. This offers a vitality that helps to nourish the physical body as well as the spirit. As we believe we are strong, so do we act . . . and we become stronger by our actions.

Self-identification is thus a facet of this chakra. While the first chakra is concerned with the sense of outright stability or security of one's self, the third chakra is more concerned with identification as it relates to the definition of oneself. Inaccurate definitions passed down through family or society often become believed, and thus stored, in this area, negatively affecting the rest of the energy system. Our own actions may then serve as a negative feedback loop, supporting this definition; or we may act in ways that break through and move us beyond such definitions, supporting a more healthy self-image. The dynamic between guilt and forgiveness is yet another way of perceiving and affecting this same process.

FOURTH (HEART) CHAKRA

Location: Chest, where your emotions tend to swell up

Color: Green

Key Words: Compassion, Bridging (Connection), Unconditional Love, Empathy

The heart chakra is usually considered to be our center of emotions. Compassion, however, has been purposely chosen as the key word here, instead of emotion, in an effort to affirm the positive, balanced expression of the heart chakra. Within the healing profession, sometimes all emotions are considered to be healthy. While all emotions are valid, and release and transformation is always a positive event when dealing with blockages, oftentimes it is important to learn to retrain ourselves regarding the emotions we move to in the first place. For example, compassion is always positive and balanced, while codependency is neither. A person with a short fuse may need to release the anger they are currently feeling, but anything less than learning to respond in ways other than anger in the first place is going to cause a situation in which their long-term healing never truly takes place.

All healers have seen a need for the release of emotions that are causing blockages—even emotionally based blockages toward feeling emotions! Sometimes the need to feel is more important than the need to "just move on," and yet at other times moving on is long overdue. As healers, we must realize when it is important to ask ourselves the following types of questions: "Am I choosing to hold on to grudges, or am I choosing the freedom of forgiveness over the constriction of hatred? Am I choosing not to feel at all, as an effort to appear more respectable? Do I believe that holding on to my pain somehow brings me benefit?" We must address these issues within ourselves from time to time in order to accurately identify and understand them within others.

Compassion is an ascended form of living and giving with emotion. While the first chakra is a connection based on groupings, and the second is based on one-to-one interaction, the heart chakra teaches us about unconditional love—a form of connection not based upon any requirements of either similarity or of interaction. Healers need to utilize this center of nonjudgment in order to work to the best of their ability. It is by setting our own judgment aside that we are able to get out of the way to let Spirit do its work. The heart chakra must be open to facilitate the best healings, and to allow the best understanding possible of one's patients.

FIFTH (THROAT) CHAKRA

Location: Throat

Color: Cobalt Blue

Key Words: Expression, Communication, Implementation

Expression is a vital part of the healing process. Without it, no act of healing is complete. Although centered in the throat, expression is not limited to vocalization. Someone who is mute may be far more advanced within the development of their throat chakra than someone who is able to speak.

Expression as it relates to healing may include counseling, crying, singing, laughing, painting, writing, dancing, praying, volunteering, playing—almost any act imaginable. Sometimes it was simply the act of expression that was ever really necessary for the healing to take place. This means that healing can be facilitated by anyone around us, whether a "professional," a spouse, a friend, a stranger, or even a child. What is imperative is that the patient is allowed and encouraged to release.

Perhaps our highest expression is the choices that we make in our day-to-day life. It has been said that our highest prayer is our life. This makes our decisions and the manner in which we execute them very powerful, and very much our own. Sometimes it is finally executing a decision that has been very difficult for us to reach that provides the greatest possibility for healing.

As the communication chakra, the health of this center greatly affects our spiritual communication, such as prayer, and the receiving of guidance or intuition. It is the first of what are known as the "upper trinity chakras" essential for this kind of communication.

SIXTH (THIRD EYE) CHAKRA

Location: Between the eyebrows

Color: Indigo

Key Words: Intuition, Guidance, Perception

As the psychic center, this chakra will continue to develop within both the healer and their patient simply due to the method of healing taking place. Development of this chakra heightens intuition and changes the perception of the world as one is open to higher truths. In healing, this is utilized as more information about the patient is accessed from within the energy centers, and from the spiritual beings present that help the healing process take place.

It is important to understand that these are not "extra" faculties, but rather their utilization is what allows us to grow further into our full awareness, as opposed to the partial awareness we have been taught to use. As such, truth about the world as it really is continues to unfold and expose itself to us, causing us to grow in power, responsibility, and effectiveness as healers.

Times in which we feel very imbalanced, cluttered, and as though we are going to burn out will either stem from or affect this chakra. It is akin to "vatta imbalance," in Ayurvedic terminology. Headaches, fever, nervousness, and difficulty in thinking clearly manifest very quickly for many people, and are usually tied at least in part to this chakra. Stress and too much input are the enemies of this chakra; meditation is its greatest friend. The pursuit of other kinds of knowledge may also be associated with this chakra, as they help make up the way in which we perceive the world. Quantum physics, mathematics, music . . . there are many ways other than the more philosophical pursuits that can help to expand our awareness of the world around us. The child with the dictionary on his lap is delving into sixth chakra territory as much the adult who is meditating in front of his shrine.

SEVENTH (CROWN) CHAKRA

Location: Top of head

Color: Violet

Key Words: Unification, Destiny, Purpose, Further Guidance

It is with this center that we connect with Spirit through the highest of our intents. In many faiths it is the throne of our soul, or the seat of our destiny. In those who are completely not aligned with the higher purpose for which they have incarnated, one will often perceive this chakra to be far off center and/or very closed. This creates a cycle; as less energy nourishes this chakra and those beneath it, it becomes more difficult to live in alignment . . . as one lives less in alignment, the chakras become even more off-center and malnourished of the downward-flowing energy provided by universal guidance.

Beginning our healing work at the head, then, is often helpful in the respect that more guidance is brought in, which helps facilitate the rest of the healing by aligning the perception with the highest guidance and understanding that we may call forth. By further opening that center, a bigger picture is more easily seen—more cosmic and less personal. On this level, there is no perception of punishment or reward, guilt or innocence, but only that of universal love continuing to try to unfold in many ways within the individual's lifetime. Thus, it is at this chakra that an individual's destiny may best be realized, and that their road to that destiny be best understood. Sometimes you will find that the sole (or soul!) purpose that the patient has come to you was really to receive this understanding, whether they knew it at the time or not.

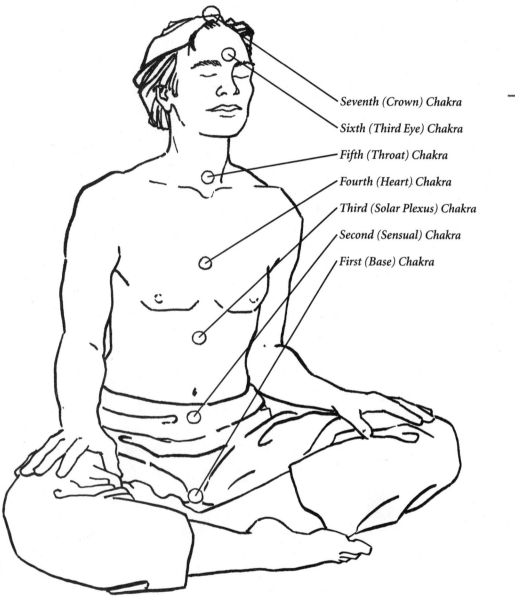

Seventh (Crown) Chakra

Sixth (Third Eye) Chakra

Fifth (Throat) Chakra

Fourth (Heart) Chakra

Third (Solar Plexus) Chakra

Second (Sensual) Chakra

First (Base) Chakra

CHAKRA MEDITATION

The following meditation gives students an idea of what it feels like to go inside the chakras within the human body by first experiencing it within themselves. This gives them the knowledge that they *can* do it when it is time to work on each other, and then on their patients. I wish I could count how many times I have told a student to utilize an ability and had them reply, "But I don't know *how.*" My reply, 90 percent of the time, is simply, "Yes, you *do.*" It's amazing what we find we can do when it is actually time to do it, and especially when we *must* do it.

The other wonderful aspect of this meditation is that it also gives each student a tool for checking in with themselves, seeing what they may need to fine-tune, or just putting or keeping themselves in balance. Continuing to work on our own energy system cannot be stressed enough. As healers, we deal with a higher influx of energy than most of the population, and if we don't want to overdo it, then we had better keep ourselves from overloading.

Before the meditation, students should be asked to sit straight in their chairs, with their feet flat on the ground, hands flat on their laps. This is called the Egyptian meditation position, for obvious reasons. The other option is to have students lying down, but this tends to make it more difficult to keep a beginner's attention from straying, especially for those who missed too much sleep the night before! Eyes should be closed, unless more experienced meditators prefer to keep theirs open. Students should be asked to slow their breath gradually *but to a pace that is comfortable to them.* Do not set an inhaling and exhaling pace for the group. Individuals who are not breathing comfortably will not be able to keep attention from their breath (or lack of it), and will not have a successful meditation. It is important that the students feel comfortable going "chakra diving" during this meditation, or they will not feel comfortable when it is time to do so with their patients.

It is time to lead the guided meditation. The voice, of course, should be soft and melodious enough to be comforting, but projected well enough for everyone to hear. Instructions have been written in regular type, dialogue in italic. Obviously, this is a guideline based upon the correspondences of each chakra, and it is hoped that Reiki Masters and practitioners will feel comfortable with experimentation in order to consistently improve the meditation and its effects. I lead the meditation to suit each group, but it is always something similar to what follows. Please note that a pre-exercise worksheet (see page 52) should be completed prior to doing the actual meditation.

Now that your breathing is slow and gentle, but comfortable, I'd like you to follow the sound of my voice. Most of us think with our consciousness located inside of our head. I would like you now to begin to move that consciousness— move your thoughts downward, descending all the way down to the base of your spine into the perineal area.

Feel and envision your consciousness descending there into a glowing, red sphere of light. Immerse yourself in that light.

Notice its shade. Are parts of it dark or murky? Or is it bright and vibrant? (Pause)

Ask the chakra what it has to tell you, what message it has to give you. It may tell you verbally, using an inner voice, or it may show you a message visually, with pictures either literal or symbolic. (Pause)

What does this chakra have to tell you about your grounding? Is this connection to the here and now something that you may want to work on, or have you managed to learn this well over the years? (Pause)

What does this chakra have to tell you about fear and insecurity in your own life? Are you good about seeing life not from a consciousness of fear or scarcity, but from love and abundance? In what parts of your life might you be able to improve? (Pause)

I would like you to imagine a beam of ruby red light coming toward you, toward this chakra. As it hits this chakra, it begins to penetrate, cleaning and clearing this chakra, and making it brighter. (Pause)

Thank this chakra for the message it has given you . . . and then begin to move upward, noticing that your environment takes on a more orange hue as you move up into the area that is about two inches below your navel. Here you will immerse yourself into a spinning, orange sphere of light. (Pause)

Again, notice the brightness of this sphere. Are there any darker areas, or is it all very bright and healthy? (Pause)

Ask this chakra what it has to share with you, and sit in stillness, ready to receive any messages it may wish to give. (Pause)

What does this chakra have to tell you about relationships? Are you good at nurturing predominantly healthy relationships? Are there others in which you are not sure what to do? Notice anyone who enters your consciousness while you are in this chakra. (Pause)

Now turn your consciousness toward your creativity. Do you feel as though you are able to utilize your creativity abundantly at work, at home, at play? What might you do differently, and where might you be able to pat yourself on the back? (Pause)

Visualize a beam of bright orange light coming toward you and into this chakra, cleansing the chakra and making this sphere even brighter. Feel it become infused with this light, growing more healthy. (Pause)

Thank this chakra for its help, and for the messages it has given to you. Say goodbye, and then slowly begin to move upward, noticing your environment taking on stronger hues of yellow. Eventually you will rest at the solar plexus, between your navel and the joining of your ribs, at a glowing, yellow sphere. (Pause)

Ask this chakra for any messages it may have about your personal strength— areas of your life in which you may need to exercise it more, or areas in which it may be best to back off and exercise it less. (Pause)

Allow this chakra now to be brutally honest with you about the topic of honor, understanding that the point is not to blame, but to simply address any issues or areas of your life in which it feels honor is not being upheld. This could be the treatment of yourself or individuals around you; it could be matters of honesty . . . anything at all. Take these messages as a positive lesson for which you can feel thankful. (Pause)

Perceive now a beam of bright yellow light coming toward this chakra, penetrating it, cleansing it, and making it brighter and stronger. (Pause)

Thank the chakra now, and begin to slowly ascend, noticing the yellow giving way to the color of a bright emerald green. We pause now at the heart chakra, the area where we feel most of our emotions well up within us. (Pause)

Allow now for the feeling of universal love to fill this chakra. Understand that all the love you have ever felt from and for others has a place here. Relatives, lovers, spouses, children, clients, or patients . . . remember those who have touched you somehow and let the feeling multiply here, and feel how the chakra grows in intensity and size. (Pause)

You have now realized the level of connection that is kept with others at the heart chakra, which is a very different level from the other chakras. Thank the universe for these positive connections, and then ask for guidance on any difficult areas you may have with anyone on this level—anyone you may want advice on how to best love. (Pause)

See again a light coming toward this chakra, in bright emerald green. Feel it penetrating and cleansing this center, helping it grow brighter and healthier. (Pause)

Give thanks to the chakra, and then move upward, slowly, into a bright cobalt blue. Rest in a cobalt blue sphere in the throat, where you feel your voice. Notice the health of this chakra, any darkness or brightness within the sphere. (Pause)

Allow this center to show to you now the health of your ability to express yourself. Allow it to show you areas of strength or areas that need your further attention regarding your expression of feelings, needs, desires . . . anything at all. (Pause)

Turn your attention now to the matter of choice. You have the strength and ability to make your own choices in life; do you actively do so? Are you proactive in expressing yourself through your choices, or do you tend to acquiesce to others? Allow yourself to be shown these answers in specific areas of your life. (Pause)

See now the beam of light returning in the bright cobalt blue color, penetrating and cleansing this center. Notice the center growing brighter and more intense in feeling. (Pause)

Thank the center for its messages, and now move your consciousness upward again. You environment turns more indigo in nature, until you reach a glowing sphere that rests between your eyebrows; it's a color like midnight blue, with a slight tinge of purple. It is an indigo blue, like India ink—a deep color that denotes a center of deep mysteries. (Pause)

Here we make way to other kinds of feelings. Remember what it feels like to know that the phone is about to ring . . . that a friend is needing you to call . . . that your dreams are messages . . . and that you are not alone in your time of need, because help is there for you, somehow, in Spirit. Remember what this awareness feels like and hold on to it for a moment, thankful for its benefit, provided for you by a loving universe. (Pause)

Think also of the other mental capabilities that you have. Do you sell yourself short of them, or are you aware of your abilities to sort things out, organize, use logic, and the many other things that we, as intelligent emissaries, are capable of doing? Allow yourself to be shown in what areas of your life you refine your spirit and your life by utilizing these talents. (Pause)

It is the middle of these extremes—the paranormal and the mundane—that is our center of existence, as we utilize both in order to be proper custodians of this Earth and of our lives. Both are equally necessary for the greatest healing of our planet, one patient at a time, beginning with ourselves. Meditate for a moment on this understanding. (Pause)

See now the indigo light coming toward you, penetrating your third eye, cleansing and strengthening this center. Give thanks to this chakra for its messages, and then realize that you are moving upward once more. Your environment becomes more violet in color, until you reach the glowing, violet ball at the top of your head. (Pause)

This is the center of highest guidance and destiny. Allow this center to show you parts of your life, from childhood until now. Be an observer of the movie as it is shown to you. (Pause)

Allow yourself to be shown, now, clues of the future—clues to where you might find yourself, what you may find yourself doing. Allow your highest guidance to come through. (Pause)

Thank this chakra for the messages and lessons it has shown you, and then give thanks for your destiny, whatever destiny it is that you chose before your birth here.

Invoke or pray now for your highest guides to be with you—angels, loved ones, whomever you feel may sometimes be of help to you. Imagine them radiating a great white light into your crown chakra, cleansing, rejuvenating, and energizing it. (Pause)

Thank your guides for being with you, helping you now as always. Say goodbye to them, and then begin to return to more full awareness of your physical body.

Feel your toes and move them a bit . . .

Move the muscles in your legs . . .

Move the muscles in your arms . . .

Move the muscles in your neck and face . . .

Move and flex and relax your body as needed . . .

And then slowly open your eyes, and take some deep breaths.

At the end of the meditation students should be encouraged, but not required, to share their experiences. Everyone will have related to parts of the meditation in some way—colors, sensations, emotions, visuals, and/or audios. The messages from this exercise, and from every other time of doing this meditation, should be used to aid in the spiritual development of each student, showing them areas of strength, areas of weakness, and guidance along their path. These are also the kinds of messages students may expect to receive when working on others.

CHAKRAS:
PRE-EXERCISE WORKSHEET

(To be filled out after chakra instruction, but before chakra meditation)

1. What chakras do I think might need the most work within me, based upon what I have learned now?

2. Why do I feel this way?

3. What issues might I expect to find there?

4. What factors in my life, past and present, do I feel may have aided in the formation of these issues?

5. How do I feel these issues may affect me now, mentally, emotionally, spiritually, and physically?

CHAKRAS:
POST-EXERCISE WORKSHEET

(To be filled out after chakra meditation)

1. From doing the guided meditation through my chakras, which chakras did I find truly needed the most work? Are they the same or different ones from what I had *logically* concluded they would be?

2. What did I find there (within those chakras)?

3. What can I do to work with the chakras that need the most help?

4. What did I learn from this exercise that should help me when working on my patients?

GIVING REIKI WORKSHEET

(To be filled out after giving a Reiki treatment)

1. How did I feel about giving a Reiki treatment before I began working on my fellow student? How do I feel now?

2. Was I able to stay relatively attentive throughout working on my patient, or did I have many things going through my mind at once?

3. What kinds of things did I find myself realizing about the patient as I was working on them? Did my patient and I end up discussing any of this?

4. Was I able to suspend judgment about my patient before the treatment? Was I able to do so throughout the entire treatment as well, regardless of what I may have perceived?

5. What about suspension of judgment after the session? Could I run into my client at a later date, and know that I will still not judge any part of them?

6. What do I think I can do to improve the sessions with my patients? What other elements may I also be able to incorporate within my treatments?

RECEIVING REIKI WORKSHEET

(To be filled out after receiving a Reiki treatment)

1. How did I feel when the session was beginning, compared to when it was finished?

2. Did I feel any sensations in any particular parts of the body as they were being worked on?

3. Did any issues to address surface at this time? Did I see any particular images, memories, or colors?

4. How might giving myself a Reiki treatment every day help, say, as a beginning or ending to each day?

REIKI HAND POSITIONS

It is important to remember that positions vary from lineage to lineage. It is also important to remember that full body treatments are not the only traditional method by which to do Reiki, although they are the most common. Working on the head, the affected site (if there is one), and any areas the practitioner is intuitively led to treat is also a traditional method. What is most important is that the patient receives the best possible session from the practitioner.

Often practitioners will remove all jewelry, even though the traditional teaching is that jewelry will not impede the flow of Reiki energy. Other practitioners will choose to wear jewelry that has special significance to them, such as items with particular crystals or stones. Each practitioner must decide what is most comfortable.

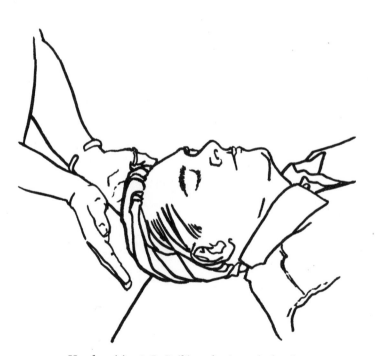

Hand position 1: In Reiki, we begin at the head.

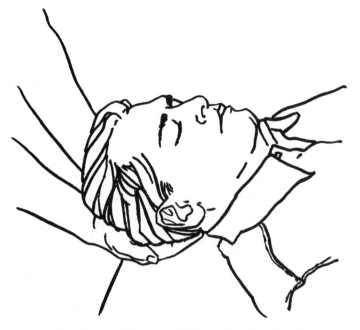

Hand position 2: Optional if using hand position 18.

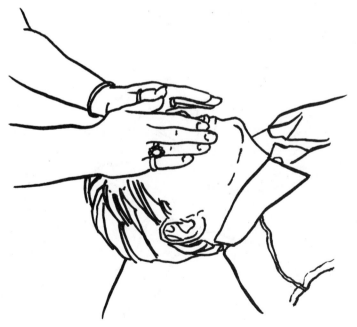

Hand position 3: The face is never touched.

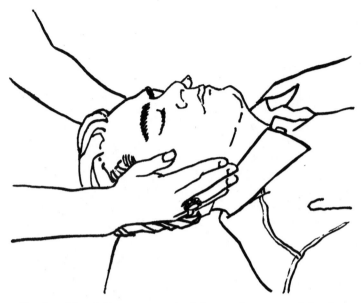

Hand position 4: Coverage area is of the temples, ears, and glands.

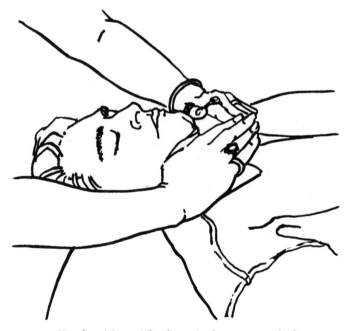

Hand position 5: The throat is also never touched.

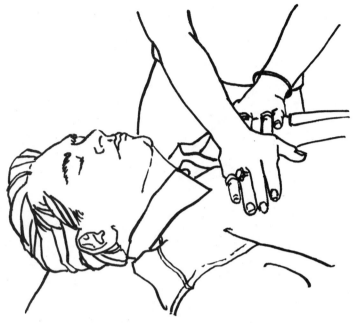

Hand position 6: The chest.

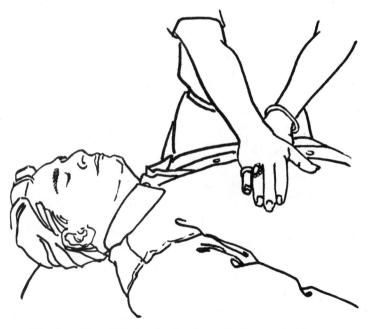

*Hand positions 7–9: Continuing down the chest and abdomen
for as many hand placements as it takes, usually two or three more.*

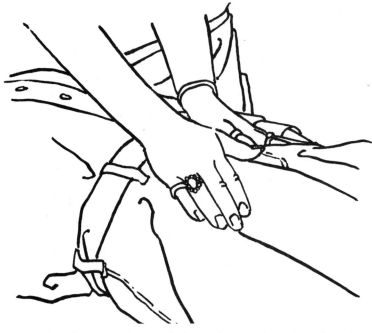

Hand position 10: The pelvic area is done with the hands in a V formation. If a patient is uncomfortable with touch in this (or any) area, remember to hold the hands off the body.

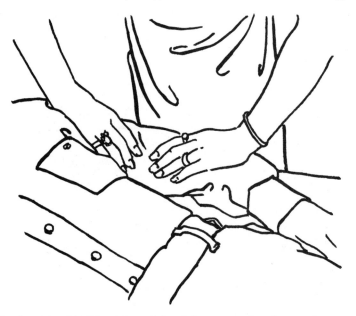

Hand position 11a: The right and then left arms are done in one of two ways.
This shows the muscles of the arm being treated.

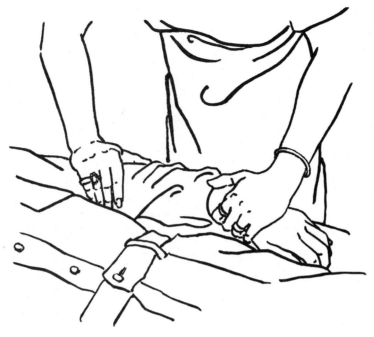

Hand position 11b: Another option for treating the arms is by treating the elbows and wrists.

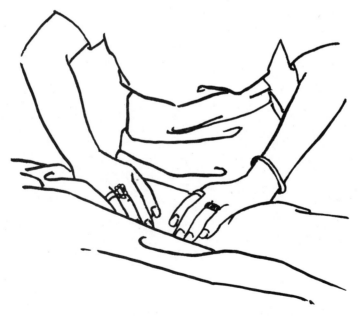

Hand position 12a: The right and left legs are done the same way.
This shows the thigh being treated.

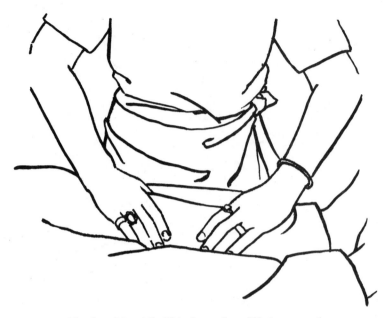

Hand position 12b: This shows the calf being treated.

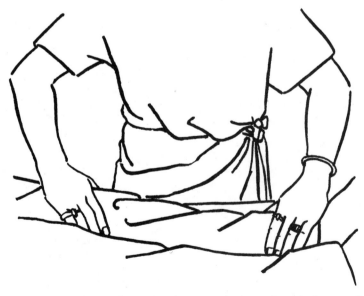

Hand position 12c: Again, another option is to treat the joints, here the knees and ankles.

Hand position 13: The feet help open centers important for grounding. Also, through reflexology, by treating the feet the entire body is treated.

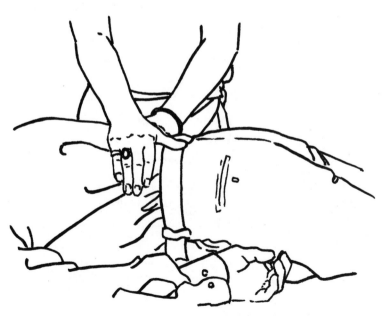

Hand position 14: The small of the back is a very important area for energy storage and production.

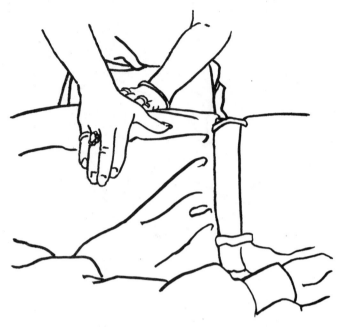

Hand position 15: Continuing up the back.

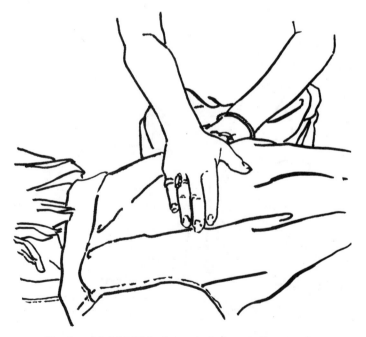

Hand position 16: This placement helps to relieve tension
below the scapulars, a very difficult place to reach in massage.

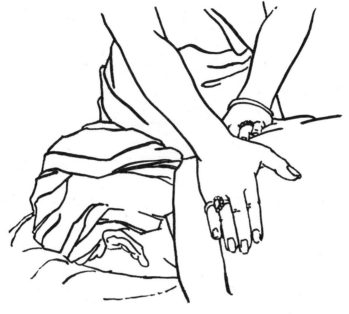

Hand position 17: Many people carry a great deal of stress in their shoulders, which this hand position helps transmute.

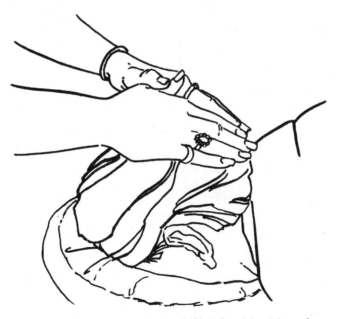

Hand position 18: Optional if hand position 2 is used.

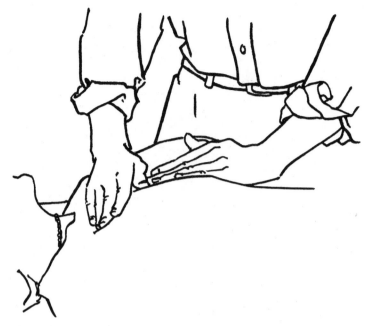

Hand position 19: The T formation is most comfortable for some female clients.

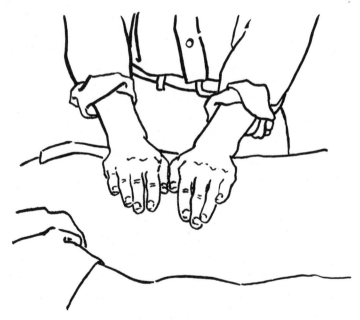

For narrower patients, it may work better to put the hands side by side,
instead of one in front of the other. This also allows two hand placements
to be done at one time when treating the front and back of the torso.

CHAPTER 6

DEGREES AND SYMBOLS WITHIN REIKI

THE VALUE OF SYMBOLS

The use of symbols predates any known use of the healing system we know as Reiki. Every culture has used them in some way, from mystical uses to everyday language. It is interesting to note that our first form of written communication is now returning to be used in an important place within the context of healing in the twentieth and twenty-first centuries. Why symbols are used in Reiki sessions is a common question, with any answer agreed upon to be "correct" difficult, if not impossible, to find.

In order to best understand and appreciate the use of symbols in Reiki, we must first change our thinking altogether in regard to the use of symbols. For example, Western society tends to view the use of symbols such as hieroglyphs as more primitive, and thus inferior, to the use of an alphabet (in itself a system of symbols for sounds) for communication. Only a complete misunderstanding of their purpose and/or a prejudice toward the cultures from which they originated could birth and uphold such a notion. From a purely physical point of view, the alphabet is convenient in its purpose. From an emotional and spiritual point of view, however, the use of symbols is vastly superior.

More is conveyed in pictures than in mere words. This can be easily illustrated by considering the ancient Egyptian symbol of the ankh. The word "life" means simply that: life. The Egyptian ankh, however, has many more layers of meaning. The *life*, the *life force*, or *eternal life* are such layers of meaning. Meditation on this symbol, as well as

Different layers of meaning may be found in symbols, which mystical teachings believe are astral keys. Symbols, left to right, from top, are AUM: *The energy that is constantly creating, sustaining, and dissolving the universe.* OROBOROS: *An ancient symbol of eternal regeneration.* THREE INTERLOCKING RINGS: *Cross-cultural symbol of deific trinities, later adopted by Christianity for the same meaning.* THE FIVE-POINTED STAR: *A symbol of five elements in both Western metaphysical teaching, and the TCM "ke" (controlling) cycle.* THE TRIANGLE: *Not only another symbol of deific trinities, but it has also become a symbol for wellness (mind, body, and spirit).* CIRCLE WITH CROSS: *Identified by different cultures as a symbol for Earth, the Four Directions, the Crossroads, or the "red road and the blue road."* ANKH: *Egyptian symbol for life.*

its sound, is revealing and powerful. It empowers with life force the person upon whom it is invoked, or any symbol with which it is meditated. Like many symbols—including the Reiki symbols—the more it is meditated upon, the more it may be understood in ways beyond words, but rather through experience.

According to cross-cultural mystical teachings, including Western and African, symbols are astral keys. This would agree with traditional Reiki teaching. In Reiki, we use symbols in order to direct the energy toward different layers of the energy bodies, for different effects. Thus we can say that, in truth, they do act as molds, forming the Reiki energy into the vibrational pattern needed to go more directly where we want it to go, doing what needs to be done.

THEIR USE IN REIKI

In the most traditional Reiki teachings, the purpose for using symbols within Reiki sessions lies in their use for the Reiki attunements. Traditionally, Reiki attunements are accomplished by placing Reiki symbols within the student's energy bodies. This links the student to the Reiki energy that is called upon by its symbols. Use of the symbols, then, takes place even by the First Degree practitioner, even though they may be unaware of the existence of such symbols! Further degrees are not a bestowing of the symbols upon the student, but rather a teaching of how to consciously use the symbols given to the student in their previously given degree. Thus, the use of symbols takes place even at the onset of the student's first Reiki experience. This and the fact that the symbols are the only method by which to pass the attunements makes the use of symbols in Reiki mandatory for its very existence.

The importance of these symbols within Reiki naturally brings us to a pressing issue within the teaching of its symbols and the way in which we view such teaching. Since its inception, Reiki's symbols have been taught in a number of ways. We know that at first Reiki students were allowed to write the symbols and keep them to study at home. Presumably, it is greed that changed this when Reiki first came to the West. Seminars were given in which students were not allowed to write the symbols, in order to help retain their secrecy. It would appear, however, that a bit too much secrecy was attained.

Playing the childhood game of Telephone, we learn all too early and easily how quickly one message may be twisted and contorted into another. The vast array of variations within the forms that the Reiki symbols are known has shown that the same process has occurred in trying to pass Reiki symbols from one generation of students to the next. The simplest of symbols have the least variation, while the most difficult can seem almost *completely* different from one lineage to another. This would lead one to believe that a lack of a consistent standard to refer to has created a situation where what is easiest to forget has suffered the most variation, due to a lack of any distinct source that one may access.

Today, students are usually allowed to write the symbols down—even encouraged to, for study and meditation. I believe this is probably best. A symbol with twenty-two or so strokes will be very difficult for a student to remember the next day! It is also preferred so that the order in which the strokes are written is not forgotten. I am aware that there are a few modern teachers who teach that the order is not important, but such teachers have obviously never taken an oriental language before. Simply by looking at some of the symbols, it is obvious that they share derivation with oriental characters, all of which have a correct order in which to be written. Tradition tells us, then, that the order in which the symbols are written does make a difference, even if the incorrect order does have effect.

OUR SYMBOLS' CONTINUING EVOLUTION

How, then, should each symbol be written? There are schools and lineages that claim to have the "only" *original* symbols. They may even advertise that those who have been attuned in other lineages can send money in order to receive the symbols as they "originally" were. As stated in the Introduction, I will not show any rendition of the symbols, or claim that my version is the only "correct" version. We are already aware that not all Reiki attunements were "originally" passed the same way. How, then, are we to believe that all symbols were always given to each student exactly the same way?

One of the most important stories I have read is a Jewish parable about an American Jewish family who was hosting a man from Ethiopia who was also Jewish. Because of the transporting of Jewish law to Ethiopia in different times and circumstances to its migration to Europe, there are some differences or variations within the writings and practices. Regarding the difference in dietary laws, the mother of the family was at a loss as to what to consider "correct" for serving within her household. When she consulted her rabbi, asking, "Which laws are correct?", his reply was, "Let the law be considered correct for each as it has been passed down by their rabbi." In other words, if both parties were following the direction of their rabbi, both were to be respected as being "correct." *This* is how I view the passing of the Reiki symbols. I cannot in good consciousness tell another that their lineage is "incorrect," especially if what they are doing has been working! It is unfortunate when this respect is not upheld and reciprocated among other lineages. The true test, then, is what works best for each student, and what they feel most comfortable with.

Another pressing point is growing within the community as well. The number of new "Reiki" symbols is growing, as quickly as new "Reiki" systems. Further degrees and symbols are those from which I shy away and do not teach. I do not take part in the learning or dissemination of such symbols or methods, because I do not believe in their professed originality. This includes claims to further degrees (beyond three) of Reiki, Tibetan forms of Reiki, or any "new" Reiki symbols. I do not condemn their claims of effectiveness, as I am not familiar with them firsthand. I am sure that they are at least as effective as any basic plan in which individuals come together for a positive, healing experience. I simply choose not to condone them or their claims. To be plain: I will use any other symbol or method which I am *led* to use within any individual session, but I still will not then teach them as being *Reiki* symbols or methods. By teaching Reiki in its purity, I allow my students to choose for themselves any modalities to further explore on their own, without diluting the Reiki teaching and tradition.

THE REIKI I DEGREE

The Reiki I degree is the first degree given in which a student is considered to have attained Reiki energy. Before this, the student may have attended lectures or listened to a friend about how Reiki works, but he has never received an attunement. Obviously, if Reiki is a frequency of Universal Life Force Energy, then the student must have already had the energy flowing within him. Anyone who is breathing has Universal Life Force Energy! It is the Reiki attunements, however, that further open the student up to channel more of the particular vibration that we call Reiki.

It is that first attunement that brings a student to the Reiki I level. A student who has been given the attunement and no teaching is still able to channel the energy. It is the attunement, not the teaching, that advances the student to each degree. It is expected, then, that each student will be given the appropriate teaching to help them understand how to best utilize their degree. Just as different symbols are used to advance a student from one degree to the next, different teachings go along with each degree.

At the Reiki I level, the student is traditionally taught only how to give a Reiki session, or treatment. The student is taught the Reiki hand positions passed down through his lineage, as well as the understanding of how Reiki works. Traditionally, no symbols are shown to the Reiki I student. In reality, this makes sense. The Reiki I level is for the basic laying on of hands. There have already been symbols placed within the student's energy centers that will work without need of conscious direction, allowing the Reiki energy to flow and do its job.

This may sound like a bit too little to learn. Perhaps this is why some lineages have begun to teach first level students one of the Reiki symbols, called the Cho Ku Rei. In reality, though, there is plenty for any healer to learn from this basic experience of laying on of hands. It is while still at this level, for example, that the student will learn about having confidence and yet letting go. Here he will face the importance of treating himself. He will find the kinds of situations in which he witnesses Reiki to be most effective, and develop his own style of healing that works best for him. He will also be asked to struggle with nonjudgment. These are in addition to all the personal issues that the attunement itself may drudge up in order to facilitate further processing and releasing by each student!

Although I do not teach the Cho Ku Rei or any other symbol to my First Degree students, I do digress from tradition by teaching distance healing. Although usually not taught until the Second Degree, when the Hon Sha Ze Sho Nen symbol is taught, I teach it so that my students will feel comfortable utilizing this part of their abilities right away. Distance healing has been practice by people of every faith, whether by symbols, prayer, meditation, drumming, chanting, or sacrifice. I prefer to teach my students how to send the energy in a very effective way from the beginning, so that if anything should happen to loved ones (or even if not!) at a distance, they would understand that they can still use Reiki to help any situation. There is a symbol taught at the Second Degree that is very helpful, but certainly not a necessity in this instance, as history and experience have proven. I encourage my students who attain the Reiki instructor/Master level to do the same with their own Reiki I students, but do not require that they have such plans, as this break from tradition is a personal choice.

Distance Healing

I teach distance healing (also called *sendings*) the same way to both my Reiki I and Reiki II students, with the exception of the use of symbols, which I teach only at the Reiki II level. I suggest trying the following:

Ideally it is best if you are able to retire to a private, peaceful space (even if it's the bathroom, for you busy parents). Either sitting on the ground or in a chair with feet flat on the ground, begin to relax. With breathing comfortably slowed down and eyes closed (if preferred), raise your hands, palms facing each other, about a foot or so apart. Between these hands, visualize the person you want to send Reiki to. If not yet very proficient in visualization, or if you do not know what the person looks like, then call up the image of a generic person—whatever comes to mind, with no details such as coloration, significant size, etc. Intent and visualization will set up a connection with the person to whom you are sending the energy, but some people also like to say the person's name a few times, until they feel the connection is stronger. If you have attained the Reiki II degree, now is also when you will utilize the distance or bridging symbol, Hon Sha Ze Sho Nen. In many lineages we are taught that there is actually a sending pattern, referring to the order in which the symbols are first utilized. It is as follows:

Hon Sha Ze Sho Nen (better establish link and bridge sending)

Cho Ku Rei (further empower above symbol and address physical)

Sei Hei Ki (address mental/emotional levels)

Cho Ku Rei (further empower Sei Hei Ki)

Dai Ko Myo (for Reiki Masters)

Next, begin sending Reiki to the image lying between your hands. Just as in a regular Reiki treatment, only intent is required to get the energy flowing. Often you will intuit areas of the body and/or issues that need particular attention. You can move your hands to concentrate on these particular areas of concern, in addition to having your hands at the crown and feet, infusing the person's entire body and aura with Reiki energy.

When you feel as though you are finished, you may close with a thanks or blessing to the person receiving the Reiki, and then quickly snap your hands away and cease the visualization. (The intent is to have as clean and complete a release as possible, allowing yourself the focus of energy needed to continue helping yourself and others.)

As I said, the ideal is to be in a private place, free of interruptions. This allows the intent and intuition to really flow. However, this is not necessary every time we want to give Reiki, either in a regular treatment or a sending. I have given Reiki while helping hospital patients walk down a hallway, touching them at the small of their back. I have also done Reiki sendings during five-minute breaks from work or studying. Holding hands is one of my favorite ways of sharing Reiki. I also sometimes secretly do sendings while watching TV, while everyone around me is unaware of what I am doing. Never limit Reiki's ability to help, even in our smallest gestures. Making time to share positive intent throughout the day is a beautiful way of life.

THE REIKI II DEGREE

At the Second Degree level, the students receive another attunement, which opens them up yet further to channel the Reiki energy vibration. My Master taught me that the leap in the amount of energy being channeled when going from I to II is about 200 percent. The leap between the level II and the Reiki Master level is about 400 percent. I don't know if those numbers are a part of traditional teaching or not, but it seems to hold some validity, based upon experience. This should not be taken as a strict rule, however, as the spiritual development and responsibility of each student make perhaps the largest difference of all.

It is at this level that the student is given the first three Reiki symbols. These symbols have already been at work within her own body. Now she is able to consciously use them to direct the energy toward specific directives within the patient's body. Some of the symbols may seem a bit difficult to memorize at first, but the more they are practiced and used, the more quickly they will become second nature to the practitioner. Perhaps the more difficult challenge is not to overdo it when using the symbols. Relaxing and doing what comes to mind is better than stressing out over which symbols to use at any given moment. The symbols are sacred, as well as being tools for us; we are not slaves to the symbols. Concentrating too much on their use can detract from our concentrating on the true purpose of the session: the patient. Letting go and not using any symbols is better than blocking the flow through frustration over trying to figure out what symbol might be most helpful. Relax, be guided.

Cho Ku Rei Symbol

The first symbol, the Cho Ku Rei, is sometimes called the empowerment symbol, activation symbol, or even the light-switch symbol. In truth, these nicknames can be quite misleading. The Cho Ku Rei is a symbol of empowerment, used to amplify both the Reiki energy being channeled and the energy of the other Reiki symbols. It is not, however, necessary to "activate" or "switch on" the other symbols. All of the Reiki symbols stand on their own, retaining their sacredness, power, and effectiveness.

The Cho Ku Rei is considered to correspond most with the physical body when used on its own. When sent after other symbols, it brings further empowerment to that particular symbol's objective, rather than acting on its own on the physical. It is because of its empowerment abilities that it is sometimes taught to First Degree students as the "light switch." In truth, the Reiki energy will begin to flow through the practitioners' hands simply by intent—and sometimes even without it! When the Cho Ku Rei is used, however, that energy is amplified and can thus be felt more easily when it begins to flow.

Some also use the Cho Ku Rei as a protective symbol against negative vibrations for both people and places, such as when cleansing the home or healing space. Others also use it for the purpose of manifesting external objectives. These uses are later additions.

Sei Hei Ki Symbol

The next symbol, the Sei Hei Ki, is used to consciously send more energy to the emotional body. Reiki already functions a great deal through the emotional body, so many situations can be expected in which this symbol may be found particularly useful. So much of our dis-ease is due to issues that we just can't seem to process or release. Some we are aware of, and some we are just as painfully unaware of. The Sei Hei Ki can be used to bring comfort and aid in processing and releasing when the issues begin to rise to the consciousness of the patient. It can also be used to help initiate the process, sending energy to the emotional body of a patient whose energy is particularly blocked on that level. We block our emotions when there is a great deal of pain or the threat of such pain. Sending healing, comforting energy can help a patient feel more safe and nurtured to begin to finally open up those areas where there is so much fear and pain.

Hon Sha Ze Sho Nen Symbol

The other symbol taught at the Second Degree level, the Hon Sha Ze Sho Nen, can also be nicknamed the bridging symbol. It bridges just about everything! It is best known for its ability to bridge space, as it is the symbol we use to better facilitate our distance healing, which is traditionally not taught until this level. Its function is broader than that, however, as it is also used to bridge time. It may be used to send healing energy back to a particularly emotionally painful time in a patient's life, or the time when the patient first started manifesting the symptoms of her complaint in order to offer clues as to its purpose. It may also be used to send Reiki energy back to times of personal dispute, in order to help transform that energy into a more harmonious energy that moves forward from that time on—an interesting way to take more responsibility for our karma!

The Hon Sha Ze Sho Nen symbol is just as effective in bridging the future as the past. It may be used to send the Reiki energy to a particular time or event. For example, if a practitioner is in a class at three o'clock on a Monday afternoon when a friend is receiving surgery, she may do a sending that morning with the intention for it to unfold either at three o'clock, or at the surgery itself. Then, after the class and the surgery, she can do sendings concentrating more on the present recovery. In this case, the symbol has been used for both of its aspects, those of space *and* time.

All of these symbols can be used either alone or in conjunction with one or more of the others. They are drawn in a variety of methods: in the air, on the body with a finger, even with the tongue on the roof of the mouth! Visualization with intent seems to be the most common method of all, and works just fine.

Reiki Box

It is at this level that students are traditionally taught about the Reiki Box. It is unfortunate that this teaching is beginning to be lost, as it is so effective in helping the practitioner to not get tired out doing sendings to everyone she feels would benefit from Reiki (which is pretty much everybody). A Reiki Box can be made from anything, from an old shoebox to a box of a more elaborate design bought or made specifically for Reiki. On the inside of the box, the symbols are drawn. Within the box, the practitioner puts strips of paper with the names of people whom she would like to send Reiki to.

She may then do a sending by holding the box and sending the energy with the intent that it goes to "all who are represented within my Reiki Box." In this way, many people may receive the full amount of Reiki energy given in a Reiki sending, without the practitioner having to spend hours exhausting herself trying to send Reiki to the same number of people one by one. She may also still do individual sendings for those whom she feels need the individual attention. From time to time, the practitioner will revise the names in the box. As names are removed from the box, the paper strips may be destroyed as formally or informally as desired. For those who wish a respectful end to them, and do not have safe burning accommodations, returning them to the strength and purity of the earth may be desired. (Of course, an all-natural paper would then be used.)

I invite those who doubt the effectiveness of the Reiki Box, as I did, to try it for just two weeks. It took half that long for me to find out just how effective it is. People who had been stuck in problems for years were consistently coming up to me and letting me know of the breakthroughs they were finally having—and they were all people whom I had put in my Reiki Box! The only explanation I can think of regarding how it works so well is the ancient Hermetic law, now called by science the holographic principle. According to Hermetic law, everything is contained by, and contains, everything else. This is likened to a hologram that, when split into any number of pieces, contains separate, complete images of the whole instead of *fragments* of the whole. Evidently, the Reiki Box works along the same lines—everyone who receives the sending receives the whole of the energy, rather than much smaller parts.

THE REIKI III DEGREE

The third Reiki degree, usually called the Reiki Master degree, is attained by an attunement somewhat different from the rest, in which a part of the Master's prana is passed on to the student accepting the degree. Three more symbols are given, as well as the ability, training, and authority to pass the attunements that create other Reiki practitioners. Before this last attunement, the practitioner is not considered to be attuned to enough of the Reiki energy to effectively pass an attunement on to another individual.

Dai Ko Myo Symbol

Of the three new symbols, the Dai Ko Myo is the symbol most used in Reiki sessions. The Dai Ko Myo is a strong symbol, encouraging wholeness on all levels. Its purpose is a bit more vague than the other symbols, and yet it is very powerful. It has been described to me as "man, woman, God, and Oneness." It has been described by others as working on the karmic level and, although I cannot think of a way to not work on the karmic level, I can see how a patient's growth would be hastened greatly by this symbol's ability to flood all the energy bodies with the God force. In its "man, woman, God, and Oneness" function, it works to unfold and bring out the higher purpose trapped within individuals who are dealing instead with the manifestation of their issues. It affects the immune system quite directly, and the practitioner is often taught an exercise to strengthen the immune system with the use of this symbol.

Raku Symbol

The Raku is a symbol that the student will use only for passing attunements. It represents the life force as it travels along the spine either slowly or very quickly. Its symbol illustrates the downward moving energy, from the transpersonal chakra into the body. It is sometimes drawn with curves, reminding one of how it spirals around the chakras. Other times it is drawn much like a lightning bolt, emphasizing a quick downpouring of this energy from above.

Antahkarana Symbol

The third symbol taught at this level is the Antahkarana. Some say it is only used for Reiki Master attunements, but I have known it to be used in more extreme situations within sessions. It is the crème de la crème of all the symbols, and can somewhat represent the purpose and ideal methodology of our practice.

Even within esoteric teachings other than Reiki, the Antahkarana has parallels. Perhaps the Egyptian ankh is one version, representing the Godforce as it penetrates and brings life and awareness into physical matter. Within Hebrew mysticism is the *Merkabah*, or "vehicle of light." This vehicle refers to the vehicle in which the undifferentiated, unmanifest Absolute descends into the manifest world. The Yorubas call it *Imole*, or House of Light. It is the spiritual place where Spirit and matter are transferred.

Within Reiki, also, the Antahkarana represents the source of all light, and the destination to where all light must eventually return—the source and destination being the same being/object/locale. We know that light travels in both particles and waves; this is the source and repository of all that light, both physical and spiritual—all the suns, all the chakras, all the stars, all the love. Where they come from, and where it all must return to make its way out again, this is the Antahkarana. This is what our symbol for the Antahkarana represents and calls upon. I have not seen the symbol in print, even in books about Reiki that claim to have printed it, perhaps due to differences in the teachings between lineages.

Reiki Master Guides

Often at this level the student is taken through a guided meditation to find his Reiki Master Guide. We all have guides that help us through the most important aspects of our lives, and we often feel that guidance quite strongly when giving and receiving Reiki sessions and attunements. This meditation may help by creating a format in which one's primary Reiki guide (i.e., a guide for utilizing all aspects of Reiki) may establish a more clear rapport. The student may or may not receive information, such as a name or what the guide looks like. This is fine. Chances are the student has already felt plenty of guidance during sessions, and this will continue. He should not feel pressured to produce results from the meditation. Guidance is very individual, both arriving and being perceived in many different ways. It could be that the student has a good deal more growth before he is able to have conscious contact with his primary guide, if that guide is already at a level much higher than what the student is used to consciously working with. It could also be that the student's guide is a consciousness that has never incarnated, and never will, into any form. This kind of guidance can seem very amorphous at first to those with a different idea in mind; in reality, such guidance can come in every bit as clearly as from a guide who has been incarnate. A lack of perceived results does not mean that the student has no guide, or that he will never feel a good connection. It simply means that at that particular time the student has not made that connection. It could still come over the next few days or, in some cases, perhaps much longer. Time does not indicate failure, only a time frame.

Students

Once reaching this level, the new Master may take on all the responsibility that goes with accepting and teaching students. Some make it easier by choosing *not* to take any students. This is perfectly acceptable. Some will wait a period of time in order to feel ready. Often the new instructor will know he is ready when the students start approaching! Each instructor is expected to do the best to his ability, be available to his students, teach the traditional methods, and to set the best example possible.

AFTER THE ATTUNEMENTS

It is a traditional requirement for students to spend a period of time after every attunement to give themselves treatments every day. The time varies, but is usually approximately a month. This aids the student in getting used to the new energy flow, and helps to make any inner cleansing happen more smoothly. Detoxification symptoms may occur, such as runny nose, runny eyes, or diarrhea. They are energy detoxifying through the physical plane, and will leave in a few days. Meditation, the self-treatments, and other forms of holistic detoxification may be used to help speed up and maximize the process.

Self-treatments are a wonderful way of life, not just for the period of time after an attunement, and not just when sick. When I'm slipping, I can feel it. On the other side, when I'm taking care to do my practicing on myself, I can feel the difference in a big way. It is a beautiful way to start each day. It is also easy to fall asleep while doing Reiki with each hand on a key area I want to work on.

Reiki is used for a number of other things, too. Practitioners are using it to energize their food before meals. They are also using Reiki on their healing implements, such as essential oils and stones. Reiki is being used for plants and animals too, not just people. Any time love can be called upon, you will know that there is a Reiki practitioner finding a creative way to implement Reiki! Students are encouraged to find new ways to use Reiki in their practice, as well as in their personal lives.

CHAPTER 7

EXPLORING ETHICS WITHIN REIKI

THE ETHICS OF TOUCH

It is important to remember that Reiki is effective without touch. Touch adds a beautiful element to the modality, and is a basic need for everyone. However, not everyone is psychologically capable of dealing with touch. It is essential that we never insist upon the touch aspect of Reiki, or push it on someone who does not feel ready or comfortable with it. Instead, talk with patients about the great effectiveness of Reiki to help them work through their issues and suggest gradually getting to the point at which they are comfortable receiving touch, as an important part of their healing.

In dealing with issues of sexual abuse, touch is an area that almost always needs to be addressed. This is an area in which Reiki is very helpful. At some point in their progress, these patients are often prescribed massage by a therapist. This helps them to overcome their trust issues, and learn to recognize touch as a healing, as opposed to threatening, experience on both the emotional and somatic levels. On both of these levels, the releases can be quite dramatic.

The Reiki practitioner offers healing in this arena as well. In fact, there is often a gap where the patient feels a great need for loving touch, but is still afraid of the experience of massage, which they fear may be overwhelming. This is where Reiki may help to bridge that gap. With Reiki, we may begin doing treatments off the body, allowing the patient to feel the much more subtle changes occurring within them, as well as the often very palpable energy between their body and the practitioner's hands. Another powerful effect is that the patient is gradually facing their fears of touch and trust simply by allowing the practitioner to hold their hands so close to the body for an extended period of time. This is all in addition to the effects that Reiki always has due to its ability to transform from the energy level outward. This includes the issues we would find within the patient's most private areas, which would not be able to receive any work through a modality that relies solely upon touch.

The touch facet of Reiki cannot be overvalued. Without touch, babies die—and in truth we all become lonely and die a spiritual death inside without this essential element of life. A client that heals through their issues of touch has healed more fully than the patient who has not yet done so. The right to choose our own rate of healing, however, is universal. When a patient visits our table, they are agreeing to face the dark, difficult areas lurking within them. Our part of the contract is a respect in return that includes not betraying their trust by pushing them at a rate of healing that *we* want for them. This robs them of the right to heal at a pace that they feel they can handle. Touch can be a major turning point in that rate for many people. Some will move from off-the-body to on-the-body in one session, while others will require several sessions. Part of this may depend on how much healing they have already done, either on their own or with another therapist. Part of it is also because we are all different, having different lessons to learn, with different ways of learning them.

It is important, then, to be open with your patient, offering your suggestions and then coming up with a plan together. This ensures that you are attempting a session that is comfortable for both of you, not betraying trust between patient and practitioner (which could exacerbate the problem immeasurably). If the patient agrees to work on the issue of touch, but states that she does not feel that she will be ready for touch during the session, then it is important she understands that this emotional state will be respected. This also serves to reinforce the fact that she has a right to expect the boundaries she places regarding her body to be respected, even though it may not have been done at some point in her past.

On the other hand, some patients may agree to allow some areas to be touched, but wish to wait until later sessions for other, more sensitive, areas. Another option would be to begin the session without touch, allowing the patient to become more comfortable with the practitioner and the process. Then, after a couple of placements, ask the patient if she is feeling more comfortable and willing to receive touch yet. Or the option could simply remain open for the patient throughout the session to say, "I'm willing to try some light touch now," while reserving the right to deny touch at any time, either in certain areas or for the remainder of the session.

It is important as healers to remember that we empower others when we respect their rights, and when we offer them choices. Also, by empowering their energy, we empower our own by the honoring that occurs at the level of the solar plexus. For many of us, it is also easiest to learn to honor ourselves by honoring others, and helping them on their journey to honor themselves.

THE ETHICS OF PERMISSION

Permission is a big issue in the metaphysical community regarding energy work being done on or for another person. The general rule we tend to hear is, "Always ask permission." I will be the first to admit that I have not always held fast to that rule. The reason lies in the understanding that nothing in this particular universe is either black or white, light or dark, good or evil. It is all relative to comparison and situation. Indeed, the gray areas are often more abundant.

For example, one of the aspects of teaching Reiki that I enjoy most is when I am able to teach it to someone already in the healing profession. These students are already going to have their hands on patients every working day of their lives. Reiki is something they can use everyday, on many people. Their work is taken to another level, benefiting both giver and receiver. What, then, of the nurse working in the intensive care unit of a hospital? Often they will be working with patients being brought back to life only through the aid of machines to help them breathe and receive nourishment. These patients are incapable of giving permission for Reiki, or any other treatment option. Should the nurses in all hospital intensive care units then withhold Reiki from these patients, even though these are the very patients who need it most? Remember that even in the dying process Reiki can offer a great deal of comfort. Physically it can reduce pain and calm overactive vital signs. Emotionally, it can help bring a sense of peace and relief. Wouldn't it be wonderful if we could all pass over in the best possible circumstances?

What of the severely mentally handicapped, who are only aware of the fact that Reiki feels good? Without the understanding that Reiki may have physical and emotional

effects in the form of releases (which they may rather not have) and expanding awareness (which can at times be frightening), are they truly capable of making an informed
consent? Is consent from someone who is incapable of understanding the effects upon
body and mind what we are speaking of when we stand on our soapbox and preach
about "permission"? On the other hand, are we to withhold Reiki from those who may
face so many challenges in this world, due to an inner circumstance of which they have
no control? Is this protection or prejudice?

Looking at Reiki from the standpoint of mental health can often be the clarifier of
our more difficult decisions. From this standpoint, if a very lonely, elderly person in
pain, with a body racked with disease, wishes no further intervention, then we understand and support the desire to go. If they fear that Reiki will draw out this process,
then we must respect their decision. Reiki is a tool we have been blessed with, but it
cannot define or designate us as healers. Healers are also those who sit with, read to,
and listen to others. They are the ones who are still there when the times are hard.
When it is time to help someone whose time has come to leave us, then we can help in
the above ways, and by helping the patient accept and view their parting in a healthy
way, as a rebirthing. In fact, it is most often *they* who can best explain this to *us*.

On the other hand, a teenager who has much to live for but cannot see past their
own despair may also choose against Reiki for at least two reasons. First, they want to
die. Second, the pain of actually healing may at first be greater than that of staying
wrapped up in their darkness. Healing is not always easy. It often hurts! But the beauty
of the light we come to at the end of the tunnel is well worth it. If it were my child, I
know that I would not withhold Reiki, and thus I could not withhold it from any other.
They have pain, but they need to live. They are here for a divine purpose.

From the mental health standpoint, the elderly person in the first scenario may be in
a state of emotional health, if they are in a state of acceptance and peace. The teen in
the second scenario, though, is mentally not well . . . as he would probably be the first to
tell us! Are we then to withhold our help due to his wishes stemming from a state of
unhealth? As healers, do we further the unhealthy wishes and choices of unhealthy people? Would we be harming them by sending them positive energy when they need it
most in their lives? Do we step back from such people because they have a serotonin
imbalance, struggle with their sexuality, have been abused, or simply have no friends?
The very youth we do not help heal today may otherwise have one day been the very

person to help others through their own healing. When we as a society will institution-
alize our youth more readily than offering them the time for any healing, supportive
touch, then how can we ask generation after generation, "What is wrong with young
people today? How can they act that way?" (Meanwhile, the youth are saying, "How can
they act that way? Don't they see what kind of world they're creating?")

The more we have a clientele of health-conscious people able and willing to come
and climb on a massage table, the more our decisions regarding permission will be
black and white. The more we start working with patients who are critically ill on any
level, however, the more we will be working within the realm of gray. Perhaps a decision
we make one day may be the opposite of the decision we would make years later, after
further experience. This is okay, as long as we are following our highest light and doing
the best we can do.

To some, the above scenarios may not seem so difficult to navigate. It would be
strange if we were given Reiki only to withhold it from those who are too sick, too
handicapped, or too clouded in depression to be able to give consent. Every practitioner will, however, run into cases within the infinite realm of gray. For example, what
are we to do if someone is seriously sick or injured, and refuses permission due to religious belief? In many parts of the country, this would be more the rule than the exception. There are still fundamentalists out there who believe that if something is from any
religion other than Christianity, then it is a harmful deception. As practitioners, do we
disrespect their religious beliefs because—in our own opinion—they are unhealthy,
narrow, and not only individually but socially harmful? To do so, after all, is to invite
more of such disrespect upon ourselves. How can we dishonor another's beliefs and
then be offended when our own beliefs are dishonored, such as when trapped by someone wanting to proselytize to us? For this is what we are doing when we set aside their
beliefs and send them Reiki anyway.

Of course, the other option would be to withhold the Reiki. But in so doing, do we
not succumb and give power to the very beliefs we know to be unhealthy? Are we not
then allowing those unhealthy beliefs to decide our actions in our lives as well? If a religious person expects me to watch them harm themselves, am I required to do so?

Most practitioners believe that clients may, consciously or unconsciously, block
Reiki. If this is true, then it is important to remember that what a person desires or
believes at a conscious level is not always the same as what they desire or believe on the

level of the subconscious. We experience this when a client willingly lies on the table, but we find we have a great layer of fear to get through before we can get very deep. They are sometimes afraid of the issues that may arise, or have sometimes been raised with certain beliefs about methods such as Reiki. Often we think we have worked through such issues or beliefs, only to find that they are still there, lurking at a deeper level.

This can occur with permission. The critically ill person who puts on a front of religious loyalty may very much be yearning inside for the help that they sense we can give them. It is also true that someone may wish to be more open-minded than they are currently able to be; or that they have a desire to heal, but at a deeper level are afraid to begin a new life without their illness. Which of these parts of the person do we listen to? To whom do we grant the authority to make the decision?

Well, which part do we think is healthier and wiser to make the decision? Is the part saying "No" part of the problem? Or is the part saying "Yes" trying to rush things? For example, sometimes a person needs to allow ample time to grieve, not just try to get over it and move on as quickly as possible. On the other hand, there is also a time for grieving to be over, allowing the memory to remain a positive, rather than negative, experience.

The more we encounter these gray areas, the more comfortable we become with navigating them. Usually we will receive what I call a "knowing" if we just sit back and listen to the silence, with no preconceived answer in mind. If we are never given more than we can handle, then Spirit must take over where our own wisdom leaves off. After all, it is allowing Spirit to work through us that we are actually trying to do.

THE ETHICS OF CONFIDENTIALITY

Confidentiality should be a given within the practice of Reiki. A patient cannot open up and work through her innermost feelings if there is fear that the practitioner will share the experience with others. Because of this, we do not break confidentiality of any session or experience, be it positive or negative. This same confidentiality extends to attunements, as well as treatment sessions. When others hear a practitioner saying, "Let me tell you about this incredible experience so-and-so had when I attuned them," they know that if something personal happens during an attunement or session, they cannot safely share it with the practitioner. Healing insights may then be lost, and trust may be difficult to find for other practitioners of the same or other modalities as well. If this behavior is witnessed, it is time to find another practitioner or teacher.

This should not prevent the practitioner from asking for helpful insights from other healers, whether other Reiki practitioners or practitioners of different modalities. I often have students come to me with questions or interesting experiences they have had with their own clients or students. Anonymity can be kept by withholding the patient's or student's name, and by not divulging any information that may give away their identity to someone that may already be acquainted with them. By coming to one another when we have questions or after experiencing breakthroughs, we help each other in our continuing education as healers. This in turn benefits the entire healing community. This also helps strengthen the cycle of not only the student learning from the teacher, but the teacher learning even more from the student. Sharing cases while respecting anonymity and confidentiality seems to be more commonplace in the allopathic community. I believe it is a wonderful lesson we may learn from them. Without respecting confidentiality, though, this tool is unavailable to us.

THE ETHICS OF COMPLIMENTARY MEDICINE

It is a source of interest and wonder to me that we live in such a varied universe. Due to this variation of individuals and kinds of dis-ease, one thing that can be said without doubt is that no one modality is right for everyone and everything. Not that Reiki can be harmful; however, certain modalities are certainly better with certain people or ailments than other modalities. For example, a back out of alignment will respond much more quickly and effectively to chiropractic than Reiki (although using both would be best). A poor immune system, however, often responds better with herbs and Reiki than with allopathic medicine.

It is because of this diversity within the interaction of individuals, ailments, and methods that we must be certain not to close our minds to any safe modality. This includes allopathic medicine. We do a grave injustice to our clients if we do not recommend a holistic approach to their challenges. "Holistic," however, does not always mean completely natural. We tend to use the two terms interchangeably, but in reality "holistic" simply means looking at the whole organism (mind, body, and spirit) and treating it from this standpoint of wholeness, as opposed to simply dissecting and treating the parts.

If we look at the world in terms of two necessary polarities, then, we see a yin and a yang, a feminine and a masculine. Traditionally, we say that looking at things in terms of wholeness and similarity is from the feminine side, or right side, of the brain. Looking at things from the parts and differences tends to be classified as masculine, or from the left side of the brain. Just as we need both sides of the brain to draw upon in order to function fully, and just as we must have a yin and a yang in order to have a fully functional universe, so, too, must our society utilize both sides of medicine in order to fully utilize our responsibility to heal.

For example, I remember when one of my first students to receive the Reiki Master degree told me that she was diagnosed with Lyme disease. She was living in the part of the country with the highest percentage of Lyme disease cases and, fortunately, was not far from where a university was conducting the most cutting-edge studies regarding this serious, and potentially fatal, ailment. She was strictly vegan, and for years had never taken over-the-counter or prescription medications. She had always relied on Reiki, nutrition, herbal remedies, and a positive attitude, with great effect. Upon learning of her diagnosis, she asked the specialists what her options were. She was shocked to find out that as of yet there were no natural alternatives found to be effective against Lyme disease. Not herbs, not acupuncture—just very strong antibiotics. And if the oral antibiotics weren't strong enough, then she would have to go on further antibiotics intravenously.

Antibiotics are a nightmare for strict naturalists. All of the care they put into establishing the positive flora in the intestinal tract, and all the electrolytes and other benefits of a healthy fluid balance obtained from drinking lots of pure water, are destroyed. So, of course, I was worried she would not submit to the rounds of medication, despite my previous lectures. To my delight, there was nothing to worry about. She realized the importance of doing what was most likely to help her (yes, of course, doing Reiki all the while!), and did so without complaint. She realized what it was doing to her body, but knew that it was up to her to get better, and then take an active stance toward building her body back up. Even better, she was not embarrassed, hiding what she was doing from others, but openly shared her experience. In this way she became a fine example to others of someone truly committed to her health.

I would like to see others more interested in opening further joint ventures between allopathic and holistic medical modalities. It is wonderful for a cancer patient to experience Reiki, but imagine the wonder of the patient as further x-rays and MRIs are able to show the shrinking of the mass. Seeing the image in front of their eyes can help build their faith, and thus aid their healing more than utilizing Reiki without the benefit of such technology.

Meditation has been used for decades in drug and alcohol rehabilitation centers. It is but one more example of holistic and allopathic approaches being used together successfully. Dare we imagine going a step further and teaching Reiki in those facilities as well, offering another modality to help these patients going through the trauma of detoxification on both the physical and emotional levels? Only a commitment to complimentary medicine by both parties can make this happen. Volunteering some of our time is a great thing to do, but we must also make a living to feed ourselves. Can we imagine funding for Reiki Masters to travel to such facilities as rehab centers, hospitals, hospices, halfway houses, and schools to teach Reiki?

A divisive mentality will not make these ideas happen. A disrespect for hospitals will keep us out of the hospitals. Looking down at possible uses for chemical or other technological intervention makes us unwelcome by physicians, and makes us look ridiculous when we end up with no other recourse ourselves. Now, more than ever, we have the opportunity to make more allies out of those who were once our staunch opponents. By doing so, it is our patients who benefit from the strongest medicine possible, and it is our responsibility to do what we can to make this available.

As Reiki practitioners, we can be at the forefront of this movement more and more as our modality gains further acceptance, because our modality is so flexible. Reiki can be utilized for both physical and mental health, and with any other modality, with virtually no contraindications whatsoever. It can also be taught easily to the patients themselves, allowing them to do self-treatments. It requires no tools, and thus can be done even while a patient is still in bed, and requires no preparation except for informing the recipient. Surely, with all this to offer, Reiki practitioners have a distinct opportunity to be pivotal in the development of the practice of complimentary medicine in the West.

— CHAPTER 8 —

THE REIKI PROFESSIONAL

CARE OF THE SELF

Other than the Reiki Principles, there are no set rules of conduct for the Reiki practitioner. Students may be, and too often are, advanced without concern toward how they practice what they know—or even what they know. In order for respect toward Reiki to grow even proportionately to the number of its practitioners, this must undergo a change. In every tradition based upon energy and the cultivation of energy, it is expected that the tree may be judged by its fruit. This includes not only the results obtained by the patients, but the effects of the tradition upon the practitioners as well. A question we may expect to hear from anyone interested in Reiki is, "How has Reiki benefited your own life?" In other words, how have we grown?

Attaining a sought-after title is not the same as growth, even if it is obtaining a goal. Feeding the ego is not the same as growth. Learning a new ability is not growth when the student has not yet learned the appropriate context in which to apply it. In a universe of polarities, there is no right or wrong action, only times and methods in which to apply those actions. As the Christian Bible says, "For everything there is a season." The difference between the sage and the neophyte is the ability to always understand the correct action (method) for the season (circumstance).

A student's (and Master's) practice of Reiki will always reflect his growth, or resistance to his growth. His outer life will reflect his inner life, because that is where the outer life begins. A practitioner who takes little care of his surroundings, practice, and time probably has little or no care regarding the energy flow within his own body either. If he were in touch with the energy within himself, then he would be sensitive to how his environment and lifestyle affect it. His patients would then not have to undergo sessions where the quality has been compromised, much like attending the performance of an opera singer who is a chronic smoker.

There is no doubt that the care-giving role of the practitioner must start with himself. The more the practitioner is in balance, the better he will function and the more open he will be to receive the guidance relevant to not only his patients' lives, but his own as well. This balance begins, first and foremost, with the practitioner's ability to allow himself to be human. If the student is looking for a way to climb upon a pedestal, he would do best to look elsewhere. It is harmful, backward, and ineffective for anyone to put others' inner balance before their own. Due to the amount of energy and responsibility he carries, it is even *more* harmful, backward, and ineffective for a Reiki practitioner. Besides that, there are so many Reiki practitioners that respect is rarely gained simply from being a practitioner of Reiki, but rather from the reputation earned by being a particularly *effective* practitioner.

The ability to be human, then, allows the Reiki practitioner to utilize the knowledge that time must be taken for herself. She does not expect herself to work among everyone else's imbalances, take time for everyone else to have sessions, and then deal with the same life stresses and responsibilities in her own life without needing to take time to rebalance and take care of *herself*. Not being perfect means being able to say, "I'm sick," when we're sick, without feeling ashamed because we're healers. When we're not trying to uphold a facade of perfection, we can say, "I'm sad," or, "I'm just feeling a bit lonely right now," if that's what we really feel. Reiki is for real people with real issues, interested in healing themselves and, sometimes, others.

Not everyone will practice Reiki as part of their profession, nor should they be expected to. No level requires this. Some people are meant to utilize Reiki only for their own growth and well-being. Others are meant to share its blessings with others in sessions. Some are meant to do these things as well as teach Reiki to others. Even some who attain the Reiki Master level will only utilize Reiki for themselves. This is fine. I have had students that make wonderful Reiki Masters who were at first reluctant because they did not feel it was a part of their purpose to teach Reiki. There are plenty of others to pass the tradition on, and not every Master will make a good instructor.

Besides, any individual who spends such time and resources for the healing of their self becomes closer to unveiling their true Self, and the whole planet benefits as a result.

SOME IMPORTANT TOOLS

For those who *do* plan to make Reiki a part of their profession, beginning with the self is always the most important issue. Once this is put into practice, a guidance devoid of ego should do the rest. Learning what has worked well for others, however, may also prove to be of benefit. This is what I have attempted to do with this manual. This chapter, in particular, is about the characteristics and methods I have found to be particularly effective when taking on the added responsibility of a professional.

We have already discussed the importance of caring for the self first and allowing ourselves to be human. Some more of the characteristics I have found essential are as follows:

- Adherence to the Reiki Principles we proclaim.

- Ability to affirm the positive regarding issues brought out in Reiki sessions.

- Ability to follow guidance, even (*especially*) when it doesn't "make sense."

- Nonjudgment.

- Respect of one's students and patients as also being one's teachers.

- Cultivation of one's own energy.

- Healthy knowledge of other modalities, and the ability to refer out to practitioners of those modalities.

- The ability to charge (not necessarily money).

- The ability to *not* charge.

- Allowing students to contact us with questions.

- The desire to *do* right, not *be* right.

- Faith.

- Nonattachment to how the results manifest.

- Accurate record keeping.

- A healthy environment in which to live and in which to have the practice.

Many of these characteristics, as well as others, are the "fruits of the tree." Their presence is an indication that the tree itself (the practitioner) is relatively healthy from more than just the allopathic point of view (which can hardly be considered an authority on wholeness). These are the qualities we hope will grow as we advance a student from one degree to the next, and after. Many are self-explanatory. We will take a look at a couple of the others so that the reader may understand why they have been included.

Keeping Records

Accurate record keeping is the last thing many practitioners think of as a topic for Reiki. Those of us who have tried it, however, see its immeasurable value. True healing takes place on all levels only when the patient can perceive their path to wholeness as a journey where the indicated lessons have been both lived and learned. Reiki makes this available because it works with mind, emotion, and spirit, as well as the body. If the sessions are seen as separate entities, then both the practitioner and patient have missed the point. Dated records that include the current indications, issues (causes), procedures, and treatment plan provide a journal and an understanding of where the indications came from, how they were irradicated, and what they mean within the context of the patient's overall life. Either every session or every three to five sessions, it is helpful to let the patient have a copy of the session/s so that they can see their progress in black and white before them. This instills a knowledge of active participation and empowerment to the patient, instead of the old feeling of powerlessness they may very well have felt regarding their original challenges. An example of how such records may be kept is in Appendix E, and is based upon an actual experience I had with one of my patients, whom I saw for only a short time. It is a good example of how Reiki can influence a patient's life greatly in even a short amount of time, and how the sessions can be accurately put down as records.

A Positive Environment

A positive environment in which to treat one's Reiki patients is of obvious importance. There are many factors that may contribute to such an environment, all with the intent to maximize the session with each patient. The appropriate music may help the patient relax more quickly and enter a level in which the Reiki energy is received deeply, with less resistance. Water may be placed for the purpose of absorbing remnants of negative energy. Stones, plants, and incense are all tools that may be utilized to create a cleansed, high vibrational field of energy even before the session begins. Opening windows to let light and fresh air in often is also important for keeping a vibrant environment, allowing stale air to be replaced with new life. Color plays a key role, as well as lighting (fluorescent being the worst). Of course, prayer and intent go perhaps the furthest of any method in creating a clean, positive environment. We can get an idea of the positive interaction of the environment and the Reiki session by creating an example:

Lisa has come to Jose for her first Reiki session. Jose welcomes her with a caring voice and genuine smile. He brings her to the treatment room, which Lisa notices is in soothing earth tones. She realizes she can feel very comfortable here.

Jose begins by asking Lisa how she came to hear of Reiki, and what she knows about it. She replies that a friend of hers began utilizing Reiki sessions to help her deal with frequent migraine headaches. Feeling that it helped, she suggested Lisa give it a try for the pain and tension she often suffers from her fibromyalgia. Her friend told her that it involved hand placement and that, like acupuncture, it was based upon the flow of energy within the body.

Jose explains a bit more about Reiki and how it works. He tells her that everyone has energy that flows through their body. When the energy flows freely and without obstruction, this energy engenders health. When there are obstacles or imbalances, we become unhealthy. Reiki is a simple way in which positive energy is channeled to correct the flow and reestablish balance within the body, mind, and spirit. Jose also makes sure that Lisa is aware that Reiki is usually, though not always, done by touch on most positions. He asks her about her comfort level with this, letting her know that hands remain stationary within each position, and that the patient always remains fully clothed. Doing Reiki slightly above the body is always an option at any or all of the positions. Lisa informs him of having no problems with the healthy use of touch, and Jose goes on to explain that at times he may incorporate other modalities, such as reflexology (in which he has been trained), in order to maximize the session's benefits. Lisa agrees with this concept.

With her consent given, Jose prepares to begin the treatment. He asks Lisa if she has any aversion to incense or essential oils, and utilizes a very light scent when she voices her agreement. He invites her to lie upon the massage table, which has been draped with a clean cloth, and offers to drape her with more fabric if she becomes cold at any time. The music he chooses is instrumental, with a flowing tempo that is soothing and appropriate to aid in calming the patient. He reminds Lisa that she need do nothing, that she may simply relax. If she wishes, she may take note of any images or issues that arise if she feels it may be helpful. Every Reiki session is different, and at times there may be great emotional release, but they are usually a very pleasant, and perhaps insightful, experience.

When the Reiki session is over, Jose helps Lisa to sit up. He leaves to wash his hands and pour her a glass of water as she collects herself a bit more. He explains that drinking some water may help to reground her, and that having a light lunch at a nearby café before returning to work may be helpful as well. He asks how she feels, and they share insights based upon what they perceived during the session. This includes letting her know which areas seemed to need more work, and what this may signify. It is Lisa's choice what insights she may want to look at more closely and what, if anything, she feels may not pertain to her as well.

When Lisa has left, Jose attends to the treatment room. Since he had two clients before her, he opens a screened window, letting in sunlight and circulating some fresh air. The fabric is pulled, and the table is cleaned. Jose looks back at his treatment room with pride and love, and then breaks for a healthy lunch.

Knowledge of Other Modalities

Knowledge of other modalities is an important point that cannot be overstated. It is important to know what modalities may work best for each patient, allowing the patient to either utilize them along with the Reiki sessions or, if needed, choose them over the initial idea to use Reiki. If I see that energy is trapped primarily within someone's soma, then I will not hesitate to suggest a modality that is primarily somatic, with respect also to the spirit. This is common, for example, in sufferers of abuse who have tried in vain to release the aftereffects of their trauma. The best way to release much of the shame is often to work *through* (not around) the body. Then the progress is much quicker than continuing the predominantly emotional work would have been. A basic knowledge of the benefits of modalities such as acupuncture, chiropractic, massage, shiatsu, rebirthing, homeopathy, herbalism, naturopathy, ritual, psychotherapy, and meditation are invaluable to the Reiki practitioner who has the patient's healing as the top priority. Reiki is one beautiful and effective method of healing but, as with all other methods, it is not the best or only method for every case that we will see. If we can save a patient time and pain by sending them to someone else, then it is important that we do so. Of course, this is almost never an either/or situation. In virtually all circumstances, the best scenario would be to use Reiki along with any other modality being used, as opposed to not using it at all.

97

Nonattachment to the Results

Nonattachment to how the results manifest is as important to the practitioner as it is to the patient. If it seems like a patient's life is going through a lot of changes, then the sessions are working. If they become unsure of themselves for the first time in their life, then the sessions are working. When their life is falling apart, it is so it can be put back together again in another way, more aligned with their destiny . . . until it is time for the next level. We cannot rush in to save all of our students and patients, and we *should not* . . . because there is nothing to save. Everything is going as it needs to for more truth to be seen, processed, and built upon. This is every bit as important as the times that students and patients feel that, finally, "Everything is becoming so much clearer," or that they feel a deeper peace than they ever have before. If we would not "rescue" the student in the latter position, then it is equally illogical to do so for the student in the former position. This is a part of our nonjudgment: not judging the patient, and not judging the method or pace in which the patient's healing takes place.

The Ability to Be a Student

The respect of one's students and patients as also being one's teachers is one of the most valuable tools we are given for our growth. Consistently we will attract students and patients for which we could say, "Wow! That person could have been me!" They are mirrors of ourselves: how we have been, what we are, and what we could be. As we uncover their own issues, we uncover our own; and as we learn their lessons, we learn our own as well. As healers and teachers, we learn from many lifetimes at once. Without proper respect of these students and patients, we would miss these lessons, and miss out on the opportunity for accelerated growth. This reciprocal growth pattern is all the more reason to allow students to continue contact for questions and guidance. It is our responsibility when we accept a student, and it is also to our own benefit.

— APPENDIX A—

THEORY FOR SOUND, COLOR, AND STONES

Spirit moves. It/He/She creates, destroys, grows strong, weakens, celebrates, and weeps through Its/His/Her creation. This is how, spiritually, we say that all things and beings have and share in this animating Spirit. Speaking in terms of physics, we say simply that "All things are in motion." We humans, more than any other known aspect of physical creation, are capable of choosing our motion and changing our vibration. Throughout the world it has thus been recognized that it is we humans who are most "created in the likeness of God." We came from the Source, with abilities much like that Source.

Our co-creative ability is mentioned biblically when it tells of man's literally God-given privilege to name all the animals created. Remember that, to ancient cultures, to have something's or someone's name is to have a power over it. This is why in some cultures children are actually given two names—one for the entire community to use, and one known only to his or her family. A name is identity juxtaposed with sound. Sound is vibration. Vibration is the power to create reality. This fact is shown us yet again in the Christian Bible when it says, "In the beginning was the Word, and the Word was with God, *and the Word was God. All things came into being through Him, and without Him not one thing came into being.*" (Italics mine.) This is but one newer spiritual and scriptural basis for the link between sound vibrations and creation. Hindu, Buddhist, and Egyptian sources go back much further, speaking of the same creative principle.

Of course, we know that sound is not the only vibration, or frequency. Color is also a vibration. Color is not a physical characteristic of any object, but rather a characteristic of light. When we perceive something to be of a certain color, in truth that object is only absorbing all the bands of colors within white light, except for the band of color (or mixture of colors) we are seeing. Change the composition of the "white" light (such as from fluorescent to sunlight) and the same item shows us a quite different variation of color. The item has been given a different composition to absorb and reflect. Our eyes will thus pick up different vibrations, decoded by us as different colors. When we perceive different colors, then, we are noticing different frequencies of light being reflected our way.

The ancients knew of this relationship between color, vibration, and creation, too. It seems that throughout the world, creation tales speak of a void before creation took place. Sometimes grades of humidity, or even movement, are described—but never light. Darkness, but no light . . . even though there is no light present to define the darkness. It is instead defined by the simple *absence* of light. Thus we can see that even thousands of years ago, the ancients knew that light had an important place in creation; to them, no creation equalled no light. Light is color, and color is light—it is simply a matter of whether or not we have an absence of light being reflected that determines our perception of blackness. Therefore, as light takes a place in creation, so too may we take its separate components (colors) and utilize them in our mission to co-create in a healthy, positive manner.

By these same principles of vibration, indigenous cultures have learned how to categorize frequencies inherent within the earth. This knowledge has then been used to aid in creating harmony and balance when disruption has taken place—i.e., healing. Our society's technology is categorized in terms of molecular structure and is usually kept quite separate from its spirituality. In contrast, this concept is alien to these cultures who have recognized that Spirit and science should, and do, quantify one another. Thus their technology categorizes by effect upon and within this Spirit. This is true not only of sound and color, but of aspects arising from the earth itself, such as its stones and plant life. Categorizing, then, was done by vibration, proven not only through the talents of each culture's "sensitives," but also through many years of experience noticing what worked when treating patients.

As we know, different stones and plants have different vibrations, or frequencies. It is these differences on the energy level, in fact, that in turn manifest as the very differences we notice physically. How they act upon the human energy field (and thus the body) has to do with what happens when we put two vibrations in close proximity to one another. We have examples of this happening every day on both large and small scales. If we choose to begin on a larger scale, we may look at the moon.

The moon is a very large body, rather close to the Earth. Its relationship to the Earth determines not only its phase, but also its effect upon women's menstrual cycles. Indigenous cultures' women, and any women spending the majority of time in nature, will have their menstrual cycle in sync with the moon. It is precisely because of this common cycle that the moon has long been a symbol of womanhood. Likewise, women who live together will often begin to cycle in sync.

Other examples of vibrations spilling over are even more obvious. The bus or train rumbling by, shaking the earth beneath our feet. The sound vibrations of the stereo speaker shaking the glass (or car) when the volume is turned up.

But subtleties can be equally powerful at transforming the reality around us. The pendulum is an easily observed example. Two pendulum-run clocks put next to each other will eventually come to swing permanently in sync, no matter how out of sync we may begin them. The actual vibrations formed by the clocks are miniscule. They do not seem to shake or move on the walls, even though the pendulums swing back and forth. Put your hand on the clock, and you can feel that it is stable. And yet there is something very subtle but powerful that will always cause them to swing in sync.

We naturally *also* exist in sync with the perfectly balanced world around us (left alone, nature does keep itself balanced), as evidenced by the examples of the moon's influence on women's cycles, birthing, and the behavior of entire societies. (The full moon's effect on birthing can be confirmed by any nurse; its effect on societies can be confirmed by any police officer.) The seasons also affect our moods—darker seasons giving way to darker moods, while lighter seasons beg us to celebrate. We are co-creators, though, and as co-creators we are vested with the ability to create ourselves, and the world around us, as a much less-balanced picture. We tend to do so in two ways. First, by removing ourselves more and more from nature, which is perhaps our strongest balancing factor. Second, by living out of anger, violence, fear, and the whole host of emotions that get trapped in our bodies and minds, creating disharmony and thus physical and mental unhealth.

It is interesting that we choose this scenario. What is more interesting, though, is that we have always had in our hands the ability to remove such disharmonies. Take, for example, someone with an imbalance of anger. The vibration of rose has a gentle, calming effect. This vibration is manifested strongly in the physical when condensed within the oil. Thus, its odor will have a calming effect when allowed entrance through our olfactory senses. Likewise, oil of lavender may be used to aid with headaches, by rebalancing energies throughout the body. Cinnamon's very fiery energy may be used to energize, while patchouli's very earthy frequency may aid in grounding a great deal.

Similarly, we may open ourselves to another source of earthly vibration—the stones. True, we do not have sensory organs for a stone's vibrations in the same way that we have a nose for scent, or ears for sound. But we do have the ability to sense on the energy level, translating the input with our bodies and minds. Ever walk into a room and get a really bad feeling that something happened you would not have cared for, like a disagreement, or someone talking about you? Ever feel really positive about someone who simply walked by you, or whom you were just introduced to, for no apparent reason? This is the same sensory ability we are talking about here—being opened up to something or someone external to you, and allowing yourself to be affected by it (or to realize that you are already being affected by it).

In this way, we find many people feeling soothed by rose quartz, opening their intuition with the aid of amethyst, learning to ground with the aid of hematite, or balancing their energies with the help of kyanite. Clear quartz has been considered sacred by cultures on virtually every continent, even though it is not particularly rare. Its ability to channel or hold great amounts of energy make it an obvious choice for many uses. Even today, our society uses it extensively in the same way (conveying energy) for its own kind of nonspiritual technology.

Returning to a spiritual and Earth-based technology—a model equally useful in healing as the Cartesian model we find in allopathic medicine today—can be best done by looking at the findings of both ancient and modern practitioners. Doing so, we find several different models that may prove useful. As examples, colors associated with the five elements of traditional Chinese medicine; tone and mantra for each of the chakras and doshas within the wisdom of Ayurvedic India; stones and herbs used by Native Americans; and natural oils used by practitioners of modern aromatherapy. It seems that everywhere we look, we can find a people with their own technology to offer, already used for healing purposes. Line drawings and mandalas from the Caribbean, Tibet, and the Americas. Rhythms, dance movement, and trance states from the nations of Africa. These are all ways that we can bypass the riffraff, cutting directly to the spirit to help correct the organism through releasing and rebalancing. There is nothing new under the sun, only expanded applications.

In the following appendices, then, is a compilation of the more common uses for some of the previously mentioned tools of our Earth's and Spirit's ancient technology. As Reiki practitioners, we are already using vibration, as discussed in the chapter "Redefining Reiki." Practitioners will find that a partnership between Reiki and any other healing modality contains the potential to be even more efficient than either modality alone. Some will gravitate more to the stones, some to colors, while others may be drawn to still practice only Reiki for awhile, focusing their concentration. I encourage exploration and experimentation as Spirit leads us. In this way we may broaden the power and scope of the healing community.

INCORPORATING SOUND WITH REIKI

The use of sound to change vibration, and thus reality, goes back literally thousands of years. The Upanishads extol the use of the mantra "Aum," probably the one mantra everyone has heard of. In the ancient tradition of Judaism, the Hebrew alphabet was given directly by God. The secrets within the scripture, hidden within Gematria, show that one can understand a whole new level of meaning when understanding the attributes of each of the letters. The power of pronunciation has not been lost, either. The Tetragrammaton, or name of God, is not allowed to be pronounced.

Entire volumes can be, and have been, written about the technology of sound. From the frequencies of sound waves and disease, to mantra used for both healing and warfare, the more one explores the scientific and ancient understanding of sound, the more one will always continue to learn. I will leave it to the reader to find further information from greater experts in this fascinating field.

In taking a brief overview of just a few forms of sound therapy, it should be understood that music therapy is actually a field all of its own. Such professionals are trained in both psychology and music. This is by no means a simple field of study, as those seeking degrees in music therapy must not only take psychology, but also master music theory (a difficult prospect for we who have problems with mathematics), and learn several instruments. This allows the practitioner to assist the patient with actual hands-on use of creating music as well as listening to it for its therapeutic effect. Obviously this is a powerful combination of second and fifth chakra work, expressing from deep within.

One of the more simple ways that we laypeople who are also healers tend to harness the power of music is simply through that act of listening to and feeling it. Sound tables can be either bought or built, allowing the music and vibrations to rise through the massage table, being absorbed into the patient's body. One may use music with a certain noted effect, or music made specifically for the balancing of the body's energy. Whether music is used through a table or throughout the room, many practitioners find its use to be essential in their work. Of everything that is being done, often the most important tool for any kind of healing session is the stilling of the mind. Relaxing the mind and emptying it of the several layers of thought we tend to have going on at one time is what truly paves the way for relaxing and emptying the soma of the equally chaotic energies. Doing this in a silent room would be difficult for many people. The addition of music facilitates this process for both the patient and the practitioner, who must be able to remain focused on her patient's energy system and behavior.

An important part of being able to utilize this ability inherent within music is to choose music with a minimum of words understandable to the left brain of the listener. This is to prevent the left side of the brain from taking hold of words and continuing the chaotic thought patterns we tend to get caught up in. By stilling this part of the mind, we are capable of inducing a state of receptivity, or a trance state of at least the alpha level. This allows us to then utilize mantra or music that may sink deeply within the awareness to awaken or release what is necessary to reestablish balance within the energy, and thus somatic, levels.

An example of utilizing mantra may be the mantra "Hum." In the *Devi Mahatmyam*, Durga (as Kali and Ambika) destroys the hordes of *asuras* (demons) and their master in part by use of the mantra Hum. When we understand that this tale of external battle is truly an illustration of the battle occurring within all of us, then we comprehend Durga as the Divine Feminine, and the asuras as our own inner demons. By cultivating the sound (vibration) Hum within the feminine aspect of our being (gestation), we are then utilizing a tool that helps us to conquer the demons of Hatred, Anger, Egotism, Greed, and a whole host that go by many other names. This sound is therefore known to purify the spirit by the disintegration of the negative through alignment with the extreme positive, much like a divine warrioress commissioned to destroy evil.

In a similar manner, one may choose music to accomplish particular purposes. Music with high, floating tones may be used to help raise awareness, or drop away the heavier energies of the day. Music with lower tones is equally useful to help us ground and really get to the roots of many problems still held within our energy and soma. Being flexible and sensitive to what energies are waiting to work with us may also allow us to take our cue as to which music to choose.

If patients comment that they seem to respond well to music, then they should be educated about how they can continue to benefit themselves between sessions. Taking time out to listen to music that aids a function they are looking for may mean incorporating it during meditation, with self-Reiki treatments, or while drifting to sleep. If the attempt is learning to relax and release, then driving in the car is the perfect time to turn a potentially stressful situation into a positive one.

Practitioners may also choose to purchase books or audiotapes about mantra. And by experimenting with mantra during sessions, each session may expand the experience of both patient and practitioner. Mantras associated with each chakra may be intoned, or a mantra may be intoned throughout the session to elicit/empower a desired effect.

Here is a list of things you may wish to try and/or encourage your patients to try:

- Using music or mantra during sessions.

- Charge a crystal with mantra by intoning the mantra during meditation with the crystal held close to your lips. Then wear the crystal for continued aid.

- With some music specifically chosen to elicit or draw out certain moods or energies, begin listening and then—when you start to feel the flow—begin painting, drawing, or coloring abstractly, as the music leads you.

- Take a bowl of pure spring water. Add some flower petals if you wish. Now, intone a mantra for healing over the water several times, imprinting the pattern upon its surface. Now use the water to cleanse yourself in a bath, dressing in white after you're done.

- Utilize the names of the Reiki symbols as mantra, choosing one for each meditation. You will gain deeper understanding of them this way.

- Try drumming while visualizing the Reiki symbols in your mind, allowing the symbols to travel directly to your subconscious.

- Attend drum circles or symphonic concerts.

- Go out alone somewhere in nature, where sounds such as traffic cannot be heard. Sit where intuition guides you. Spend an hour or so just listening to the sounds of nature. This works well to rebalance and recenter.

- Either in addition to, or instead of, other methods of cleansing such as smudging, cleanse your treatment area or home with mantra and a small bell.

- Encourage patients to build up or loosen blocked chi through spontaneous movement, dance, Tai Chi, or Qi Gong, with music.

Practitioners and patients may easily come up with their own ideas. If one method doesn't feel quite right, don't be afraid to try another one. Play and experimentation are a part of healing, too.

INCORPORATING COLOR WITH REIKI

Color is another versatile tool, and very easy for patients to feel comfortable using on their own. There are many models available, with some variation regarding the effects and correspondences of colors. Some of these models are the TCM model, the chakra system, the Kabalah, the Orisha, and astrology, as well as cultural tradition. Within this book we have already covered the color correspondences of each of the chakras. Here is a list of some other common color correspondences, as used in healing:

Red: Invigorating, vitalizing, heating

Yellow: Self-image/confidence, joy, inner strength

Orange: Creativity, energizing mixture of red and yellow

Browns/Earth Tones: Grounding

Green: Refreshing, nourishing

Light Blue: Cooling

Medium Blue: Calming, mothering

Dark Blue: Mystery

White: Cooling, cleansing, clearing and protecting

Gold: Reenergizing at a higher vibration, contact with higher beings

Silver: Protective, cleansing, antibiotic

Pink: Loving, opening to emotions

Bright Purple: Transmutation, spiritual growth

Black: Extremely grounding, contracting, cloaking

Color is used in a number of different ways. Although many who do energy healing will try to project energy of a particular color, it does not make sense to do so within the context of practicing Reiki. It is within our teachings that Reiki is an intelligent energy that already "knows what to do." We only get in the way when we try to intervene with our limited view and attempt to impose our own will. Reiki renders this step unnecessary, and cumbersome at best.

Some ways in which color can be used to augment healing of yourself or others by adding them to treatment sessions or day-to-day life are as follows:

- Painting the treatment area a color that is flexible to aid many kinds of healing. Soft colors often help to soothe and comfort patients who may be seeing you for the first time, and may be unsure of what to expect.

- Covering the treatment surface or client with fabric of a particular color.

- Wearing predominantly a particular color for a few days.

- Taking baths of a particular color. For example, in espirituál, baths of a blue color are often taken by adding a little bit of bluing to the water. White baths are often made with powdered milk, and simmering rose petals often creates a green cast to the water.

- Imagining a certain color filling your aura and body during meditation or relaxation. Practice breathing the color in and out through the pores of your body.

- Meditating on the chakras, visualizing each in their corresponding colors.

- Light therapy is sometimes used by sitting in a room that is lit a particular color.

- Practice projecting energy of a certain color with friends, taking turns between giver and receiver.

- Meditate on one color per meditation. Then write your experiences in a journal.

- Go to the museum. Notice how different colors make you feel as different shades, tones, and textures were utilized by the masters for different effects.

To really understand color, one must play with it and experience feeling it as much as possible. Reading books on color uses and the psychology of color just doesn't do the trick in itself. See which patients respond well to color, and encourage them to experiment and give you their feedback as well. This will also give you a bigger picture about how many people respond to color in similar ways.

INCORPORATING STONES WITH REIKI

As unbelievable as the use of stones may be for some people, it is amazing how many of them—once they try it—are surprised at how much they feel they have responded to them. Again, sensitivity, respect, and experimentation are the best teachers, but there are a few helpful pointers to remember about the use of stones.

SHAPE

The shape of the stone *does* make a difference in its use. For example, a crystal that terminates without chips or breaks at one end is perfect for directing energy along the flow of the crystal, coming out the side of the termination. A crystal terminating this way at both ends is called a double-terminated crystal. It is excellent for receiving and projecting energy at both ends. (This also makes it perfect for placing between two other stones within a layout in which you want to facilitate the flow between both stones.) A smooth, tumbled stone will have the effect of radiating its energy in a more spherical manner. This is the basic on shape, but the more one knows about the various formations, the more one is able to utilize the stones' latent abilities. For example, stones may also have windows, keys, records, bridges, phantoms, and more. These are all formations on or within the stone that are manifestations of the properties it has in addition to the properties of other stones of its kind.

CLEANSING

It is important to cleanse your stones between clients and, if you buy them, after purchasing them. This is not for the purpose of feeding paranoia or possessiveness. Stones, like everything else, absorb the vibrations of everyone and everything around them. A stone used during a session, then, has absorbed much energy that was released by that patient. We do not want to then pass that energy on to another person. Likewise, a stone handled by many people in a store should be cleansed of the many chaotic energies already within it. Some of the more effective ways of cleansing stones include leaving it in strong sunlight for a few days, soaking them in strong saltwater, smudging them with sage, burying them for a while and, of course, doing Reiki on them.

DOING A LAYOUT

Layouts are usually done by placing the stones on and/or around the body based upon the action of the stone or its correspondence with an energy center on the body. For example, amethyst is often used on the third eye in order to facilitate work associated with that chakra, such as the growth of intuitive guidance and insight. Amethyst is known for that ability, and so it is placed on the corresponding chakra. A scepter crystal, often used for getting to the root of an issue, would be placed wherever we feel a particular problem may be stored most within the body.

CLEAR QUARTZ

Clear quartz is considered the master crystal. Theoretically speaking, one could do an entire layout with only this stone. It is even considered by some energy workers as the solid version of light itself and, in fact, is the best stone for bringing a lot of light into a particular area. It is also the best for transmitting energy clearly, and magnifying it. This is not the only reason clear quartz is so venerated, though. It is also the programmable stone. This means that it can be programmed to aid the undertaking of any purpose, as opposed to the other stones, which have their own finite properties. When the stone is cleansed the programming is cleansed with it, so it may be programmed with either the same, or an entirely new, purpose.

Here is a list of some other commonly used stones, and a brief overview of their correspondences:

Amethyst: Development of intuition and spiritual growth; great for absorbing headaches

Malachite: Heart chakra, emotions

Rose Quartz: Calming, inner peace through love

Azurite: Development of intuition, communication

Obsidian: Protection, grounding, cutting energy cords

Hematite: Blood problems, emotional grounding

Tiger-Eye: Solar plexus, strength, confidence, vitality

Garnet: Cleansing and energizing of each chakra

Forest Crystal: Tuning in to nature

Bloodstone: Protection, development of personal power

Boji Stones: Balancing energies of body

Pyrite: Strengthening and patching of energy field

Mica: Growth through recognizing flaws and strengths

Pearl: Opening to emotions, birthing

Geodes: Growth of hidden gifts

Labradorite: Upper chakras, cosmic consciousness

Lapis Lazuli: Wisdom, connection with the stars

Calcite: Augmenting energy of chakras of corresponding color

Citrine: Cleansing

Kyanite: Alignment of chakras and central energy channel

Amber: Sexuality, communication with nature

Some healers will end up with a large collection of stones, which can be quite expensive. I recommend starting small, and expanding gradually by acquiring what you and your patients seem to be drawn to most. Use of the stones is an extremely enriching experience, teaching us the abundance of healing energy that Mother Earth so freely gives to us. It also teaches the value of diversity within the Oneness, and how we may all benefit from celebrating in it. Your stones become dear to you, and you often know when it is time to pass one on, or which will be your lifetime friends.

— APPENDIX E —

EXAMPLE RECORDS

27 June 2000
Smith, John
Session #1

John has had T cell count of 70, high virus count, and respiratory infection for several weeks now (lungs currently at 70 percent capacity). Is on many medications, which cause chronic digestive problems, as well as steroids that have been effective against wasting. John has been trained in meditative and visualization self-healing techniques, and is receiving a form of bodywork with a body/spirit outlook.

At crown chakra, fear issues regarding fulfillment of purpose in this state. Issues of identity at navel center. Lungs took a great amount of energy from both front and back, as did solar plexus and second chakra. Energy flowed very easily along blood flow . . . something to utilize even more, once the more acute problems are out of the way.

Plan of Action: Strengthen hara and tan tien in order to build the strength and energy needed for the body to finally heal itself, especially of respiratory difficulties. Of course, direct supersaturation of lung area also to be continued. Distance healing to be sent to him between sessions.

Told John to work on gradually deepening his breath in meditation (which he is already doing!) in sync with visualization of light coming into and healing his lungs, as a form of autosuggestion. Also have him taking a bit of time in increments throughout day to work on breath, in order to better facilitate the replacement of lost prana through his breath.

Although John has some fear arising at times, I feel confident in his recovery, and his own healing practice as a major part of that recovery. Will see how he is doing in a couple of weeks or so, to see when his body is ready to receive the Reiki I attunement (do not want his body to deal with the detoxification symptoms right now). This will allow self-treatment between sessions here, and the ability for him to treat others, as his comfort level dictates . . . aiding in his ability to further acquire and maintain his health.

—J. Tompkins

29 June 2000

Smith, John

Session #2

John came in looking very rough due to poor digestion caused by his medications; he reports that he takes 20 pills TID (three times a day). Breathing sounded a bit better, with less fluid. Is receiving more IV antibiotic tomorrow.

Session began very differently from last time. Immediately upon moving to crown chakra, my hands began to buzz very strongly. I could clairaudiently hear the vibration of it. I perceived that there were thought energies that needed balancing/adjustment. Upon moving my consciousness into John's, I perceived very old (beginning at childhood) issues dealing with his father, which physiologically are affecting his body's ability to heal, supporting the energy cycle of it turning upon itself. At the end of the session, John confirmed these issues, and I suggested that he look into the possibility of counseling. This would facilitate the releasing of the energy contributing to that process.

Upon asking him what he was doing differently to facilitate such a strong energy response in the beginning of the session, John responded that he was able to quickly go into a meditative/hypnotic state and use visualization to draw the energy into his body and revitalize different areas.

Front of lungs took much less energy this time, and energy structure is much better; the only thing holding back more rapid healing is lack of energy in chakras two and three to provide the energy source for such healing . . . on physical level translating to poorer digestion and fatigue. Not storing energy . . . it moves right through him about as quickly as he gets it. Much more energy work done on back than in front, including a good deal of trance work, done well off the body, much of it at template level. (John had forgotten father issues had come up, in counseling, in relation to his healing many years ago in California.)

Plan of Action: Support work done on lungs. Bolster strongly pitta and other energy at chakras two and three. Research possible herbal/dietary solutions to Norivir side effects on digestion (upon checking with doctor), while changing energy signature at intestines. See if milk thistle may help prevent possible liver damage caused by medications.

—J. Tompkins

3 July 2000
Smith, John
Session #3

John came in looking better this time, with lungs sounding significantly better. Over the weekend, he had a release regarding the abuse issues found last week, through talking about them with his lover. Had a terrible "medicine day" with extreme cramping, vomiting, etc., on Saturday, but then felt much better on Sunday. Today a rotation nurse came to watch our session and ask questions about it, and John was very open about his life and health history.

Very open in head area, so less work was done there. Lungs much better . . . well on the energy bodies, just waiting for the physical bodies to catch up, so reinforcement was done on the template level. (John confirmed that his doctor had told him his lungs are up to 85 percent capacity now.) Much of what was in the throat chakra was released, so the talk with his lover obviously did help. More is still stored in the heart chakra, and will eventually make its way up to the throat for further releasing.

Energy transfer between heart and solar plexus was not healthy—issues in heart chakra negatively affecting sense of self-worth/self-image in very deep self, while issues in deep self continue to hurt heart chakra as emotional center/emotional "brain." Special attention to second chakra—was reinforced/strengthened with Reiki at front. John responded well to energy work done at feet, as usual. Much more energy work was done at back entrances of chakras than front. Utilized Qi Gong at second chakra/Gate of Life area and third chakra to strengthen. Trance work done at back again.

Plan of Action: Work on digestion to get energy back for health, strength, and proper assimilation of food. Put on probiotics when done with antibiotics. Much work on kidney system will still have to be done for quite some time. John has been given some notes to study in preparation for a Reiki I attunement. If his progress continues to go so well, the attunement should follow rather soon.

Supplementation: Gave John a pitta-balancing tincture. It has herbs not only good for digestion, but for kidney and liver. Suggested he get a calcium/magnesium supplement with 500 mg to be taken TID, chewed or crushed if in hard pill form, to try to alleviate chronic diarrhea.

—J. Tompkins

6 July 2000
Smith, John
Session #4

John looked like a typical "medicine hangover" morning, but not nearly as bad as his previous one. Temporary energy therefore compromised, but stored energy still building. Complained that night sweats have returned, and of pain in left chest area, probably due to workout, yesterday and day before, but gone today. He will have his blood work done Monday, 10 July, and will have his lungs checked. Will go off antibiotics then, if lungs check out okay.

Head area very open except for congestion in nasal and sinus areas, where there was obvious physical congestion present as well. Some balancing of right and left sides of energy field also done here. His intuition and guidance are about to open up further if he allows. Unfortunately, he cannot get deep sleep, as his digestion awakens him every hour and a half or so, making communication via dreams very difficult. I strongly received the information that it is time for his Reiki I attunement.

A great deal of work was necessary at heart chakra, even more so than before. Even more is building to be released. Solar plexus is also still needing transmutation of negative misconceptions of self. Energized tan tien with Reiki.

In contrast to last session, much less work was done on back than on front. I attribute this to a growing awareness on John's part to his issues and how they are affecting him; and many of them are now naturally emerging from the subconscious to the forefront of his consciousness. This is good, so that further and final processings may be attained, although it may require inner transformations, which may be difficult to go through. Less Qi Gong done at Gate of Life/kidney network, but a great deal of Reiki done there. Some trance work throughout at finish.

Plan of Action: Reiki I attunement Tuesday, 11 July. Need to continue work at both heart and solar plexus chakras for purging and transmutation that is necessary. Continue strengthening of tan tien/kidney network. Talk to John about balancing left and right sides of energy field, and perhaps becoming too yang or too yin at times in response to different kinds of stimuli.

—J. Tompkins

11 July 2000

Smith, John

Attunement to Reiki I Degree

Attunement was remarkably uneventful for both John and myself. I purposely, however, did add one of the symbols normally used to pass the attunement to the Second Degree within his second chakra. This was a guided action, as well as one that makes logical sense to me, feeling that further development of this chakra may aid in digestion and energy level. As the action was led by the guides present, I do not question it.

—J. Tompkins

13 July 2000

Smith, John

Session #5

John appeared a bit mediciny, as usual for 9:00 A.M. for him, but otherwise looked very good. Energy system definitely gaining strength and clarity. John has noticed changes in overall better health, but has had neuropathy of hands and feet return over the last couple of days. After his attunement on Tuesday, John noticed some pain occurring in second chakra area that continued for the next day, but is gone today. Also has bouts of emotions coming up and wanting to cry, triggered by very small, "trivial" things, which John attributes to childhood feelings wanting to be released. In one instance John was at home and thus allowed the full release to occur; the other times he was in public or around those whom he felt would be uncomfortable, and thus he suppressed those emotions. He has been talking with someone knowledgeable in this area whom he feels helps him in this respect. John has approached a program about receiving acupuncture, and is expecting to receive an answer today.

Session was rather uneventful . . . everything much more open and flowing. Still extra work done on connection with solar plexus and heart chakras, and on lower tan tien and base chakra for strengthening of energy. A lot of activity still occurring within second chakra. Consolidation of energy still needed for second chakra . . . large amounts of energy still being lost, perceived on energy level as constant downward flow out of the body. Obviously his digestion/elimination system is a physical counterpart to this. Feet very blocked for the first time, and more will need to be done with them next session in order to further reopen those energy centers.

Plan of Action: John's sessions can be lessened to once a week now that he is no longer in critical condition, and may do treatments on himself between sessions here. Since I will no longer be practicing in Jacksonville, he will continue his sessions here with another practitioner. I believe that acupuncture is a better modality for aiding in the consolidation of chi that John needs in his tan tien and kidney system, and will help with the neuropathy as well. I encourage him to take a proactive stance in following up with receiving the acupuncture through the wellness program, and see it as the perfect compliment to the Reiki work that he will be receiving. The fresh perspective that the new Reiki practitioner will have to offer may be very helpful as well, particularly as John is clearing out so well, and is ready to enter the next level of his healing process.

In closing the notes of my professional history (although short) with John, I must say that I have no doubt that John will prove to be a powerful healer for others as well, whether it simply be through talking with others, or actively doing Reiki work on them at some point, perhaps through a wellness program. This is a step not only beneficial to those whom he helps, but by far for his own healing and sense of purpose and fulfillment as well.

—J. Tompkins

RECOMMENDED READING

The following is a list of books that I feel would be helpful in the library of many healers. If it seems odd that there are so few books listed about Reiki, then that is because I (and most Reiki Masters/teachers) find that there are relatively few authors out there putting out books that are particularly both accurate and helpful. To be fair, though, I am very picky. The books about Reiki that I have listed, I believe to contain some excellent information that would enrich any Reiki practitioner's relationship with Reiki as a whole. Notice that not all books listed pertain to Reiki. The intention is to help the reader explore sources of knowledge about other modalities and energy system models as well.

REIKI

Barnett, L., and M. Chambers. *Reiki: Energy Medicine.* Rochester, Vt.:
    Healing Arts Press, 1996.

McKenzie, E. *Healing Reiki.* Berkeley, Calif.: Ulysses Press, 1998.

Kelly, M. *Reiki and the Healing Buddha.* Twin Lakes, Wis.: Lotus Press, 2000.

Petter, F. A. *Reiki: The Legacy of Dr. Usui.* Twin Lakes, Wis.: Lotus Light, 1999.

———. *Reiki Fire.* Twin Lakes, Wis.: Lotus Light, 2000.

Usui, M., and F. A. Petter. *The Original Handbook of Dr. Mikao Usui.*
    Twin Lakes, Wis.: Lotus Press, 1999.

OTHER TOPICS

Balch, P. A., and J. E. Balch. *Prescription for Nutritional Healing*. New York, N.Y.: Avery, 2000.

Beinfield, H., and K. Efrem. *Between Heaven and Earth: A Guide to Chinese Medicine*. New York, N.Y.: Ballantine Books, 1991.

Brennen, B. *Hands of Light: A Guide to Healing Through the Human Energy Field*. New York, N.Y.: Bantam Books, 1987.

———. *Light Emerging: The Journey of Personal Healing*. New York, N.Y.: Bantam Books, 1993.

Chia, Mantak, and Maneewan Chia. *Fusion of the Five Elements I*. Huntington, N.Y.: Healing Tao Books, 1989.

Chopra, Deepak. *Ageless Body, Timeless Mind: The Quantum Alternative to Growing Old*. New York, N.Y.: Harmony Books, 1993.

Lawless, J. *The Encyclopedia of Essential Oils*. New York, N.Y.: Barnes & Noble Books, 1995.

Melody. *A Kaleidoscope of Crystals*. Richland, Wash.: Earth-Love Publishing House, 1991.

Myss, C. *Anatomy of the Spirit: The Seven Stages of Power and Healing*. New York, N.Y.: Three Rivers Press, 1996.

———. *The Creation of Health: The Emotional, Psychological, and Spiritual Responses that Promote Health and Healing*. New York, N.Y.: Three Rivers Press, 1998.

Myss, C., and C. Shealy. *Why People Don't Heal and How They Can*. New York, N.Y.: Three Rivers Press, 1998.

INDEX